About the Author

Buckner B. Trawick is Professor of English at the University of Alabama. He received his B.A. from Emory University and both his M.A. and Ph.D. from Harvard University, where he has undertaken additional study on a Ford Foundation Fellowship. Prior to his present position, Dr. Trawick held teaching positions at Clemson College, the University of Mississippi, and Temple University. He is the author also of *World Literature* (2 vols.) in the College Outline Series and of *The New Testament as Literature,* now in preparation.

IN*the beginning God created the Heauen, and the Earth.

2   And the earth was without forme, and voyd, and darkenesse was vpon the face of the deepe : and the Spirit of God mooued vpon the face of the waters.

3 And God said,* Let there be light : and there was light.

4   And God saw the light, that it was good : and God diuided † the light from the darkenesse.

5   And God called the light, Day, and the darkenesse he called Night: † and the euening and the morning were the first day.

THE FIRST FIVE VERSES OF GENESIS

From the first edition of the Authorized (King James) Version of the English Bible. Printed at London in 1611. Original in the British Museum.

COLLEGE OUTLINE SERIES

THE BIBLE
AS LITERATURE

OLD TESTAMENT HISTORY
AND BIOGRAPHY

BUCKNER B. TRAWICK, *Professor of English*
University of Alabama

BARNES & NOBLE, INC. N. Y.

PUBLISHERS • BOOKSELLERS • SINCE 1873

This book is an original work (No. 56) in the original College Outline Series. It was written by a distinguished educator, carefully edited, and produced in accordance with the highest standards of publishing. The text was set on the Linotype in Caledonia and Bulmer by the Wickersham Printing Company (Lancaster, Pa.). The paper for this edition was manufactured by S. D. Warren Company (Boston, Mass.) and supplied by the Canfield Paper Company (New York, N.Y.). This edition was printed by the Wickersham Printing Company and bound by Sendor Bindery (New York, N.Y.). The cover was designed by Rod Lopez-Fabrega.

Preface

The Bible is one of the most fascinating books ever written, and sometimes one of the most puzzling. This Outline is an attempt to catch and to share with others some of its fascination and to help solve some of its puzzling passages. It is hoped that the book will prove useful to the average lay reader, as well as to the student primarily interested in the Scriptures as literature.

This volume deals primarily with the historical and biographical sections of the Old Testament and the Apocrypha, beginning with Genesis and going through I and II Maccabees. Although the principal emphasis is on *literary* rather than religious or ethical qualities, any significant discussion of Biblical literature necessarily deals with content as well as technique; and it must offer interpretations of some of the content. A determined effort has been made to bring to the reader a compendium of the most up-to-date scholarship on the Bible which will be of value and interest to Protestant, Catholic, Jew, or skeptic; several points of view are presented on controversial matters.

In the belief that the King James Bible is still the best *literary* version, that has been chosen as the basis for this book. It is hoped, however, that readers who prefer the Douay, the Revised Standard, or the Jewish version will find the Outline equally helpful.

B. B. T.

Acknowledgments

The author of this outline is grateful to The Macmillan Co. for permission to quote four extensive passages (acknowledged again in the footnotes) from Mary Ellen Chase, *The Bible and the Common Reader* (rev. ed., 1952) and from George Sprau, *Literature in the Bible* (1932); and to the Abingdon Press for permission to use the maps on pp. 88 and 118.

Table of Contents

MAPS

1

Palestine and Its People

Palestine, the home of Biblical literature, is not much larger than the state of Maryland in area and population. Never the seat of a major military or political power, it has nearly always been dominated by one or another mighty neighbor. From the time when the Pharaohs controlled the Mediterranean world down to the era of the Caesars, successive foreign cultures were pressed upon its people, who, nevertheless, persisted in maintaining distinctive national customs and, above all, allegiance to their traditional religion.

BIBLICAL PALESTINE
AND THE MEDITERRANEAN WORLD

Forming part of the eastern coastline of the Mediterranean Sea, Palestine (the land known to the ancient Hebrews as Canaan) extends only about 150 miles from north to south and, at its widest, only about 100 miles from east to west. It is bounded by Lebanon and Syria on the north, Jordan on the east, and the Sinai Peninsula of Egypt on the southwest. Its total area is not more than 11,200 square miles. In Biblical times it was almost encircled by larger and stronger nations. In the ancient world it was subjected, in turn, to the great Egyptian, Assyrian, Babylonian, and Persian empires.

Egypt. Egypt developed an advanced civilization in ancient times which shed a cultural influence on the Hebrews. The Egyptians attained a high level of accomplishment in literature, architecture, sculpture, painting, mathematics, government, medicine, and military science. Their *Book of the Dead*—a collection of prayers, formulas, and charms written at various times prior to the fifteenth century B.C. and designed to sway the decisions of

1

Osiris, Judge of the Dead—reflects their worship of the gods (particularly Osiris and the sun god Ra) and their belief in personal immortality. According to some historians, Egyptian ideas and institutions affected the culture of the Hebrews, who, in due time, rejected the multiple deities in favor of monotheism.

Assyria and Other Countries of the "Fertile Crescent." Northeast of Palestine is the "Fertile Crescent," an arc of fertile lands (watered by the great rivers) extending along the eastern Mediterranean through Syria, thence eastward and southward to the Persian Gulf, thus including the richly productive area between the Tigris and Euphrates rivers. Here the settlers had access to the great seas and to Egypt.

Like the Egyptian civilization, the Sumerian, Assyrian, Babylonian, and other civilizations of this fertile area were of great antiquity. Sumerian leadership in the southern region declined late in the third millennium B.C.; the Babylonians (originally the Semitic group called Amorites) gained the ascendancy but were conquered by the Hittites and Kassites in the eighteenth century B.C. The northern region was dominated by the Assyrians, who formed a great empire that reached its peak during the reign of its last famous ruler, Assurbanipal (669-626 B.C.). The extensive library of that monarch contained not only numerous official documents but also myths, legends, hymns, prayers, proverbs, early scientific records, and accounts of battles. The poetry resembles that of the Hebrews in its use of proportion, balance, and parallelism. The Assyrians were skilled in law, sculpture, and architecture. They were militarily strong enough in the seventh century B.C. to challenge the armies of Egypt. They achieved a high level of practical skill, exemplified, for instance, in their fine system of roads. Their main contribution did not consist of creative or practical works, however, but rather of the transmission of Sumerian and Babylonian culture to the Persians, Greeks, and Romans. Some of the Old Testament stories—the Creation, Adam and Eve, and the Flood—can be traced back to these ancient cultures; and some portions of the Hebrew legal code may have been inherited from the Babylonian code of Hammurabi.

In 612 B.C. the Chaldeans destroyed the Assyrian Empire. They conquered Israel and carried the Jews off into captivity in Babylonia. Following the death of their most gifted king, Nebuchadrezzar, in 562 B.C., however, the Chaldean Empire went into a rapid decline; Babylon was captured by Cyrus of Persia in 538 B.C. (Cyrus had conquered the short-lived Median Empire which had been built up by Cyaxares, 625-585 B.C.) Under Cyrus the vast Persian Empire reached from eastern Persia throughout southwestern Asia to the Aegean and Mediterranean. The Persians conquered Egypt in 525 B.C. and then attempted in vain to subdue European Greece.

Greece. Greek culture attained its zenith in the fifth and fourth centuries B.C. The spread of that culture was given new impetus when the Greeks defeated the Persians early in the fifth century B.C.; shortly after Alexander the Great had conquered Persia in 333-331 B.C., Greek civilization, including the language, was forced upon the Hebrews of Palestine, as it was upon the peoples of other parts of the Persian Empire. Thus Hellenic culture, particularly Greek philosophy and drama, was reflected in the thought of the Jews and early Christians as well as in that of the Romans.

Greek

Rome. Roman influence was not felt in Palestine until the last Greek resistance to the Roman legions ceased in 146 B.C. In addition to serving Western civilization as a transmitter of Greek culture, Rome contributed numerous scientific and technical innovations, a remarkable legal system, and effective political organization. Roman civilization is reflected in the New Testament, where we may observe many instances of the Caesars' genius for government and for enforcing law, order, and payment of taxes.

Rome

Almost encircled by these great powers was the small but tough Hebrew nation, becoming a part of one mighty empire and then of another, absorbing culture from each, yet preserving many of its own customs and traditions and fiercely maintaining its allegiance to the God of Abraham.

IMPORTANCE OF GEOGRAPHY TO BIBLICAL LITERATURE

The location, soil and topography, and climate of Palestine had a profound influence on the intellectual and material life of its inhabitants.

Location. The location of Palestine was of great strategic significance in ancient times. It lies athwart the land route between Africa and Asia; to the west is the Mediterranean, and to the east the vast Arabian Desert. Hence any invasion by land of either continent by an army from the other required passage through Palestine. Because it was small and comparatively weak and because it was a <u>bridge between two continents</u>, Palestine suffered from numerous military expeditions. From the middle of the eighth century B.C. until the beginning of the Christian era, it was overwhelmed by one world power after another. It is not surprising that the most persistent prayer of its inhabitants was for deliverance from the indignities and persecutions to which they had been subjected.

However, <u>frequent military invasion</u> was not the only result of Palestine's unique position. The road over which armies traveled was also a <u>commercial route</u>, one of the most ancient on record; and the Hebrews had the opportunity to <u>learn a great deal</u> from the civilizations whose caravans crossed their land.

Soil and Topography. A study of the soil and topography of Palestine discloses striking contrasts. The coastal region and the narrow strip on each side of the Jordan River Valley are exceedingly <u>fertile</u> (a land of fruits, olives, wheat and other crops, "a land of milk and honey"), whereas east and south of the Jordan lies the desert, and much of the area between the Jordan and the Mediterranean is <u>hilly and rocky.</u> Some of the hilly region is high above sea level; Mount Hermon rises 9,052 feet, and Mount Lebanon 10,059 feet. But the Sea of Galilee is 680 feet below the level of the Mediterranean, and the Dead Sea is 610 feet lower than that! From its source the Jordan descends 3,000 feet before emptying into the Dead Sea. Jerusalem, only twenty miles from the coast of the Dead Sea, is 4,000 feet higher than the level of water. During the Roman era, the central hilly section of Palestine included Judah—this was the southern portion extending to Beersheba; Israel—this was the middle section extending north to the plain of Esdraelon; and Galilee—this was the northern area.

The relatively poor, hard soil facing many of the Hebrews in the large hilly area was felt to be a severe handicap challenging their utmost energy and ingenuity, both as individuals and as a people. The Old Testament reflects the courage of this bold, enterprising "chosen people" and their faith that God would bring justice to them and help them to overcome hardships. Continued misfortunes were interpreted as merited punishment for misbehavior.

Climate. The climate, too, is one of contrasts. Over most of Palestine the *rainy season* lasts almost half the year. The "early" rains, which begin about the end of October, are intermittent and rather light at the opening of the season but heavier through February. The "latter" rains begin in March and end in the middle of April; these are principally severe showers. The average rainfall is about twenty-four inches. The *dry season* starts about April 15 and lasts until the end of October; almost no rain falls during this period. Occasionally a drought lasts as long as two years. In the hilly sections of the country, hail and snow are common in winter.

The winds in Palestine are important influences. There are two principal kinds: "regular" and "irregular." The "regular" winds come from the Mediterranean. In winter they are usually from the west or southwest, and they bring rain. In summer they are more likely to come from the northwest; then they bring no rain but do help to mitigate the intense heat. The "irregular" winds are siroccos, usually from the east (the word *sirocco* literally means "east wind," but has been used to designated any desert wind). These come chiefly in the spring and blow for a day at a time, bringing clouds of sand and scorching droughts.

The temperature in Palestine, as might be expected, varies greatly—from one section to another, from one day to another, and from one season to another. In some places the thermometer has been known to rise from 48 degrees at dawn to 92 at mid-afternoon.

Such contrasts in fertility, landscape, and climate are reflected in many places in the Bible.

JEWISH HISTORY AS TOLD IN BIBLICAL LITERATURE

Modern historians have little record of when the Hebrew people originated or when the Hebrews first entered Palestine. Apparently they were nomads or semi-nomads through many centuries in Arabia (or possibly northern Egypt) and migrated into Syria, Palestine, and the Fertile Crescent perhaps as early as the second or third millennium B.C. Biblical historians started with Abraham when they sought a definite founder of the Hebrew nation. (The ancient Hebrews must have had notions of time very different from our modern concepts of centuries and millennia. Since little is known about their views of time, we can only guess what they had in mind in setting forth a chronology which seems inconsistent or illogical to us.)

The Hebrew Claim to Palestine; Enslavement of the Hebrews in Egypt. At some time between the twenty-first century B.C. (Biblical chronology) and the sixteenth century B.C. (a favored archaeological date), Abraham wandered from Ur in Chaldea to Haran in the northern part of the Arabian Desert near the Euphrates and then traveled from Haran southwest to Palestine. Genesis confirms the recent evidence of archaeologists as to the Chaldean origin of Abraham,[1] and the Hebrew language shows many Chaldean elements.* According to Genesis the land of Palestine was given to Abraham and his descendants by divine covenant. He and his people took possession of the right bank of the Jordan; but a generation later the family of his grandson Jacob was driven by famine into Egypt, and their descendants were eventually enslaved. Biblical scholars doubt that all the Hebrews migrated to Egypt; a few even consider the sojourn in Egypt to be in some respects legendary.[2] Yet, it is entirely reasonable to assume that large numbers of the people were driven by drought and famine into Egypt and were estranged from their kin who remained in Palestine.

Exodus and the Conquest of Canaan. According to the Bible, Pharaoh, the Egyptian king (probably Rameses II, *c.* 1290-1224 B.C.),[3] oppressed the Hebrews so cruelly that they eventually fled from Egypt—600,000 soldiers and their families if we are to accept Exodus 12:37-38—under the leadership of Moses and his brother Aaron. According to some modern Biblical scholars, this event may have taken place about 1200 B.C. during the reign of Merneptah, successor of Rameses II. (A fragmentary inscription by King Merneptah on a granite stele at Thebes contains in hieroglyphics a reference to the defeat of the Israelites and the curbing of the Hebrew nomads.) The Hebrews probably did not become a nation until the Exodus from Egypt. After a generation of wandering in the wilderness, they finally reached Pales-

[1] For this and all succeeding notes indicated by raised numbers, see pp. 157 ff.

* See W. F. Albright in H. H. Rowley, ed., *The Old Testament and Modern Study* (London: Oxford University Press, 1951), pp. 6 ff.

tine. There they were confronted by the hostile Canaanites and, somewhat later, the Ammonites, the Midianites, the Philistines, and other unfriendly tribes. During this period of warfare the military leaders Joshua and Gideon were the rulers of the Hebrews.

The Period of Theocracy (c. 1200-1020 B.C.). When they had achieved some degree of peace, the Hebrews placed themselves under the rule of "judges," who were at once religious and military leaders. But religion came first, and all rulers had to be subordinate to God, obedient to his laws. Each of the twelve tribes maintained a large measure of autonomy. The last theocratic ruler was Samuel, a lover of peace. But the war against the Philistines created a demand for a king who would unite the military forces of the tribes.

The United Kingdom. About 1020 B.C., Saul, of the tribe of Benjamin, was proclaimed king. Although he was not recognized as sovereign by all the tribes (possibly only by Manasseh, Ephraim, and Benjamin), he extended his rule to the lands of the tribe of Judah in the south and also eastward across the Jordan. An able military commander, Saul led his followers successfully against many of their enemies, including the Ammonites, Amalekites, and Philistines. His reign lasted until about 1000 B.C.

Saul was succeeded by David, who is said to have ruled for about forty years (c. 1000-c. 960 B.C.). He was a great warrior; after a series of brilliant victories over the Philistines, Moabites, Ammonites, and Edomites, he established his capital in Jerusalem and ruled over most of Palestine and much of the territory across the Jordan as far north as Damascus.

Note that although a king might sometimes designate his successor, the decision was always attributed to divine action. Women were automatically excluded from kingship.

David's son Solomon succeeded him about 960 B.C.; like David, he also is said to have ruled forty years. Among Solomon's foremost contributions were the building of the Temple at Jerusalem and the expansion of industry and commerce; he brought the kingdom to its highest peak of splendor.

The Divided Kingdom. Upon the death of Solomon in c. 922 B.C. (some authorities say 935 B.C.), the kingdom was divided. Solomon's son Rehoboam levied such heavy taxes that the ten northern tribes refused him allegiance; they recognized Jeroboam (a former administrator who had plotted against Solomon) as their king and set up a capital at Shechem. This northern realm was thereafter known as the "Kingdom of Israel." The southern realm, made up of the tribe of Judah and part of the tribe of Benjamin, was called the "Kingdom of Judah."

The history of the Northern Kingdom, Israel, for the next two centuries is principally a record of assassinations, usurpations, and minor wars. Jeroboam I, a strong king, held the throne about twenty years. By encouraging the worship of idols he diverted attention from the Yahweh-worship at the Temple in Jerusalem. Another important ruler, Omri, strengthened his political position by bringing about a marriage between his son Ahab and Jezebel, daughter of the king of Tyre. As Jeroboam had done, Ahab and Jezebel espoused the worship of alien gods in Israel; thus they aroused the antagonism of the prophets Elijah and Elisha, who helped to foment a revolution which led to the end of the Omri dynasty. Jehu, a new and able but most severe ruler, temporarily put an end to the worship of foreign deities. (His slaughter of idol-worshipers was denounced by the later prophet Hosea as an immoral act.) He established a dynasty that ruled about a century (842-c. 745 B.C.). His two sons were incompetent rulers, but they were succeeded by Jeroboam II (786-746 B.C.), who extended the boundaries of Israel and brought it great prosperity. Unfortunately, prosperity and luxury, combined with new customs and religious views imported from abroad, led to dissolute living and numerous social and economic evils, especially in the northern and western regions of Palestine. In vain the contemporaneous prophets Amos and Hosea warned the people sternly against the prevalent immorality.

The five weak successors of Jeroboam II did little to improve the degenerate society. Consequently in 722 B.C. the Assyrians under Shalmaneser V (727-722 B.C.) and Sargon (722-705 B.C.) found it an easy matter to overthrow the Northern Kingdom and to destroy the capital, Samaria; the following year about 27,000 Israelites were carried into captivity. The kingdom of Israel never recovered from the effects of this disaster.

Meanwhile, the kingdom of Judah, its semi-nomadic people strengthened by generations of hardships, danger, and austerity, had continued under the Davidic dynasty, which was destined to endure until the destruction of Jerusalem in 586 B.C. After Rehoboam's severe regime (c. 922-c. 915 B.C.) little of significance occurred until the reign of King Jehoram (c. 845 B.C.), who married Athaliah, the daughter of Jezebel and Ahab of the Northern Kingdom. Upon the death of both Jehoram and his son Ahaziah in 843 B.C., Athaliah seized power and murdered all but one of the sons of Ahaziah; Jehoash alone was saved, and he later became king (c. 837 B.C.). His son Amaziah waged a disastrous war (c. 790 B.C.) against the kingdom of Israel, in which Jerusalem was partially destroyed.

During the forty-year reign of Amaziah's son Uzziah (or Azariah), c. 783-c. 742 B.C., Judah's fortunes were restored. When the Assyrians threatened Palestine, Uzziah agreed to pay tribute and thus temporarily saved his kingdom from the fate of Israel. King Hezekiah (c. 715-c. 687 B.C.) allied himself for a time with Egypt and the Philistines, but later reversed this error and resumed the payment of tribute to Assyria.

Toward the end of the seventh century, Assyria's power began to wane. The Babylonians captured Nineveh from the Assyrians in 612 B.C. and shortly thereafter began to exact tribute from Judah. In 598 B.C. King Jehoiakim, making overtures to Egypt, refused to continue such tribute, whereupon the Babylonians invaded Judah and captured Jerusalem (597 B.C.). They made Jehoiakim's brother Zedekiah king, but he, too, attempted to enlist the aid of Egypt, whereupon the Babylonians returned, this time to destroy Jerusalem and carry off many of the inhabitants of Judah into exile (586 B.C.).

Palestine under Foreign Rule (586 B.C.-A.D. 125). The exile lasted until 536 B.C. when Cyrus the Great of Persia, having conquered Babylon in 538 B.C., allowed the Hebrews to return to their own country. They completed the restoration of the Temple in 516 B.C. Palestine continued under Persian rule for about two centuries. In 444 B.C. Nehemiah received permission to rebuild the walls of Jerusalem. It is also believed that, under the leadership of the priest Ezra, a large contingent (about 1,800) of the exiled Hebrews went back to Jerusalem early in the fourth century B.C.

Alexander the Great defeated the Persians under Darius III at Issus in 333 B.C. and soon brought Palestine within the Macedonian Empire. Despite bitter resistance by the Hebrews, the Greek language and Greek culture superseded their own in some respects; even the Hebrew Scriptures eventually had to be translated into Greek (c. 250 B.C.) for the benefit of those Hebrews who could understand no other language.

When Alexander died in 323 B.C., his realm was divided, and Palestine fell to the Ptolemies, kings of Egypt. In 198 B.C., it was transferred to the kingdom of Syria, ruled by the Seleucids (the Macedonian general Seleucus and his descendants). When Antiochus IV (Epiphanes), the Syrian king from 175 to 163 B.C., made vigorous efforts to Hellenize the Hebrews, the priest Mattathias and his five sons (especially the eldest, Judas Maccabeus) led a successful revolt (167-160 B.C.). By 142 B.C. the Hebrews had not only won religious freedom but also regained almost complete political independence. The Maccabeans (or Hasmonaeans) held the throne until 67 B.C. Then internal squabbling which had been going on for decades finally led to the successive intervention of the Syrians, the Egyptians, and the Romans. Judea became part of the Roman province of Syria in 63 B.C.

Needless to elaborate, the Hebrews were unhappy under Roman rule. Their unrest flared into open revolt again in A.D. 66. Rome stamped out the revolt and destroyed Jerusalem in A.D. 70. Thus ended the hopes of the Hebrew people for religious and political freedom—during Biblical times.

ECONOMIC AND SOCIAL BACKGROUND OF BIBLICAL LITERATURE

The first people to whom the term *Israelites* may be applied—the people governed by the patriarchs Abraham, Isaac, and Jacob —were a semi-nomadic tribe who lived chiefly in tents, who raised herds of sheep and goats, and who moved about as the need for pastureland or the pressure of hostile neighbors dictated.

With the passage of time in the Promised Land of Canaan (which they conquered about 1200 B.C.) the Hebrews became more sedentary, continuing their pastoral economy but devoting more attention to agriculture. Under Samuel (1060-1020 B.C.) and in the United Kingdom (1020-922 B.C.) agriculture and trade flourished. The principal crops included honey, olives, barley, figs, grapes, apples, onions, garlic, melons, cucumbers, beans, and peas. The main exports were lumber (especially fir and cedar), copper, and iron.[4] Fishing became a significant occupation. Palestine's location on the caravan route from the Euphrates

Valley to Egypt led to a brisk commerce with Mesopotamia and Egypt, and trade with neighboring Phoenicia was substantial. Commercial activity made possible the growth of such busy cities as Jerusalem, Damascus, and Samaria. The small trades and crafts and the manufacture of simple articles prospered.

The earliest society had been patriarchal, the father having had almost absolute power over his wife and children. (Some limitations developed prior to the eighth century B.C.) Polygamy had been customary in the patriarchal era, and the practice persisted into the Divided Kingdom (divided in 922 B.C.); but after the eighth century B.C., it became less and less common, so that by the beginning of the Christian era it was comparatively rare, though it was not officially declared illegal for the Hebrews until several centuries later.

Periodically under the judges and kings, recurrent economic and military crises, attributed by the Hebrew prophets to lax morality, induced the people to return to their faith in Yahweh. As each crisis receded, the moral influence of the prophets declined. Conditions of life were hard; when the perils were overcome so that the nation survived, the people attributed their survival to divine intervention.

During the unified monarchy, taxes for the Temple were heavy, forced labor was employed, and foreign artisans were imported to aid in building. Skills and techniques were passed on to successive generations. There is evidence that in the Divided Kingdom, too, there was an advanced material culture—soundly built houses with drains and cisterns, sleeping quarters upstairs, and land set aside at a distance for the cattle. Asses remained the chief means of transporting goods and people. Oxen were used in ploughing and threshing. Brisk trade necessitated the increased use of writing, particularly during the eighth and seventh centuries B.C. The continued leadership of the Temple priests through the centuries has been well established by archaeological findings (the stamped jars and coins identified by E. L. Sukenik as probably belonging to the Hebrews of Judah under Persian rule in the third to fifth centuries B.C. have been regarded as evidence that heavy taxes were paid in order to support the Temple). The Dead Sea Scrolls discovered in recent decades attest to the persisting conflict between material interests and the traditional codes of conduct.

THE RELIGION OF THE EARLY HEBREWS

The orthodox view is that monotheism originated with the early Hebrews, was expounded in the teachings of Moses, and was reinforced and elaborated upon by the later prophets. An evolutionary theory holds that there was a continuous development of the Hebrew religion, perhaps from animism to a belief in one just and merciful God who promised personal immortality.[5]

The Concept of God. Some scholars who reject the orthodox view point out that the earliest Hebrew conceptions of God's nature were strikingly similar to those of other primitive religions and postulate that the Hebrews may have been at first animistic and polytheistic. They assert that the geography of Palestine was favorable to polytheistic ideas—that, prior to the times of the great teachers and judges, the varied landscape and topography and the changeableness of the weather encouraged the animistic belief that a different deity or spirit lived in every mountain stream, every wind, and every thundercloud.* It is a fact that many other tribes who lived in the same general area (for example, the Phoenicians and the Canaanites) were polytheistic.

If the evolutionary view of the Hebrew religion is correct, why did the Hebrews turn early from the idols, the "abominations" of the Egyptians, to the belief in a single God? It has been suggested that they brought monotheism with them from the Arabian Desert, a land with little variety and few changes. Another theory is that observation of the evil consequences of idol-worship (practices such as human sacrifice, for example) induced them to reject the polytheistic beliefs of their neighbors. Their concern with morality, it is said, may have led them to believe in one God as the embodiment of goodness, the source of all

---

* A trace of animism, according to this view, may be preserved in the Hebrews' use of the phrase *El Shaddai* ("God Almighty" or "The Highest"), found in Genesis 17:1, 28:3, and other passages; this phrase could have referred originally to a mountain deity. See James Muilenburg, "The History of the Religion of Ancient Israel," *The Interpreter's Bible*, I, 297. There are many Biblical references to the Hebrew worship of (1) bull images (Exodus 32:1-35, I Kings 12:28); and (2) Canaanite *baals* (nature deities) in "groves in every high hill, and under every green tree . . . And . . . in all the high places" (II Kings 17:10-11). For other specific examples, see Joshua 23:12; Judges 2:13; II Kings 23:12-28; and Jeremiah 2:20, 7:29 and 31, and 17:2.

ethical values, the merciful and just Creator who ruled heaven and earth in accordance with his preconceived plan. The orthodox claim made by both Hebrews and Christians that God directly revealed his nature and his will to chosen spokesmen contrasts sharply, of course, with the various theories ascribing monotheism to the influence of geographical factors and a long historical development.

The Hebrew faith in Yahweh,* rejecting the alien belief in plural gods as the powers that controlled the heavenly spheres, sent the rain, and caused lightning to flame through the clouds, conceived of God as the Supreme Judge of human worth, reward and punishment, and destiny. God was not only the Creator of all things but also the directive cause of historical events. The people had to look, therefore, to God for guidance, justice, and mercy. (For example, in Chapter 18 of Genesis, Abraham pleads with God to spare Sodom if only ten righteous men can be found in that city. Men could appeal to Yahweh, a deity who could be influenced by the sacrificial offering of bullocks, lambs, goats, and doves, as recounted especially in Genesis, Exodus, Leviticus, and Deuteronomy.)

The constant military struggles of the early Hebrews led to the conception of God as a warrior, a conception shared by other primitive cultures (compare Ares of the Greeks and Thor and Woden of the Germanic peoples). Defeats at the hands of their enemies persuaded the Hebrews that Yahweh used the Assyrians and other invaders, just as he used the forces of nature, as a means of punishing his people.

The earliest Hebrews thought of Yahweh as a tribal God who was interested particularly in them, and who had made with them (that is with Abraham) a Covenant to the effect that he would prosper them as his Chosen People if they would worship only him and obey his commandments. The Mosaic God was a deity who could be found in more than one place (e.g., in Egypt or on Mount Sinai) and who set forth a definite religious code

---

* The name *Yahweh* (or *Yahveh*) is made by supplying vowels to the ancient Hebrew word which in our alphabet is written as *YHVH*, known as the "Tetragrammaton." Its true, original pronunciation is uncertain, inasmuch as ancient Hebrew was written without vowels (a fact discussed below, page 18). The name *Jehovah* has become a popular variant because of its use in the American Standard translation.

of law. He was described as being jealous of other deities, wrathful, and sometimes arbitrary in his gifts and in his afflictions which he brought upon men. Always he was holy and to be revered. During the era of the judges and United Kingdom, the priesthood and Temple organization were established to create respect for (and guide the people in worship of) the one God. Over the centuries the concept was ennobled in eloquent descriptions, with emphasis on the attributes of universality (see Amos and Jonah), justice (see Amos especially), and mercy (see Hosea). The "Unknown Prophet" (author of Isaiah 40-55) suggested the idea of a vicarious sufferer who would atone for the sins of mankind. Persecution by other nations impelled the Hebrews to yearn and pray for a deliverer, a Messiah ("Anointed One") who would overcome their enemies by force and set up a God-fearing empire. Eventually, when further armed resistance against Rome seemed futile, some Hebrews ceased to hope for a temporal, earthly Messiah and placed their faith in a spiritual, heavenly one. It remained for the Christians to teach that Jesus Christ was the incarnation of the Deity, sent to earth as the long-expected Messiah.

The Concept of Immortality. From the earliest times the Hebrews placed comparatively little emphasis on the idea of personal immortality. Their predominant belief was that God rewards people for their good deeds by giving them health, wealth, a long life, and happiness here on earth; and he punishes them here for their evil deeds by means of physical and material adversity. It is noteworthy that the Old Testament story of the Flood differs from the Babylonian Epic of Gilgamesh in that the latter, polytheistic account explains that Utnapishtim (who is comparable to Noah of the Old Testament story) acquired immortality hitherto possessed only by the gods. To be sure, the Old Testament used the word *Sheol* to designate a place or a state beyond the grave, an abode of souls neither especially pleasant for the good souls nor painful for the wicked. Occasional references (as in the Psalms) are made to the possibility of everlasting life: "for there the Lord commanded the blessing, even life for evermore." But the conception of heaven as a reward for the righteous and hell as a punishment for sinners receives its major emphasis in the Apocrypha and the New Testament.

2

The Nature, Origins, and Contents of the Bible

The word *Bible* means "little books." The term is ultimately derived from the Greek *biblos*, "book" (originally "papyrus"); the diminutive of *biblos* was *biblion*, "little book"; the plural *biblia*, or "booklets," passed through Medieval Latin into the Old French *bible* and Middle English *bibul*.

We may regard the Bible as an anthology of ancient Hebrew and early Christian religious literature, as two or three books (Old Testament, Apocrypha, and New Testament), or as a unified, single work of literature. The Bible consists of from 66 to 81 books, according to which of several versions is accepted. The Hebrew Scriptures contain only what Christians call the "Old Testament"; the Catholic Bible contains a number of books which are omitted in most of the modern Protestant Bibles. Written in three languages—Hebrew, Aramaic, and Greek—by scores of authors over hundreds of years, the Christian Bible exhibits many different literary genres and styles.* Yet it has essential unity, based on its point of view, characteristic linguistic tone, and serious dignity; for such reasons, and because of its traditional presentation as one continuous work, we *feel* that the Bible is one book. To some extent, throughout the long period of transmission of the Scriptures, the various compilers, editors,

---

* Nearly all the books of the Bible (exceptions are parts of some of the Prophetic books, Luke, Acts, and certain Epistles) are anonymous; insofar as modern linguistic and textual science can determine, most of the books bear the stamp of revisions throughout the ages. Each of the authors was devoted to his cause; some attributed their work to a great name of the past. Thus we have the Gospel "according to" St. Matthew, with no claim that Matthew wrote it but only that it is in accordance with the teachings of that apostle.

15

and translators may have brought about a degree of uniformity in the style and language of the particular version accepted by them. In the main, however, unity depends upon a certain "mode of thought" [1]—an earnestness, an intensity, a simplicity, a brevity, and a warmth—which is characteristic of all parts of the Bible and binds them together.

This unity of mode suggests a unity of purpose. For the Old Testament that purpose is to record the Hebrews' continuous quest for God—his nature, his will, and his plans—as a basis for the teaching of divine law and morality. Every mood and every condition of human life—sorrow, joy, loneliness, companionship, love, hate, conspiracy, falsehood, truth, loyalty, heroism, cowardice, war, peace, kindness, brutality, hunger, luxury—all are depicted in simple, direct terms as part of the divine stream of history, teaching the lessons of the past as admonitions, sermons, and guides for all who will listen.

CLASSIFICATION OF THE BIBLE
FOR LITERARY STUDY

For purposes of religious instruction the following traditional arrangements of the Scriptures have been widely accepted; for purposes of literary study, a classification based on literary types has been generally adopted.

Traditional Arrangements. For the Hebrews the Holy Scriptures consisted of twenty-four books arranged in three parts: (1) the *Law* (*Torah* in Hebrew), made up of Genesis, Exodus, Leviticus, Numbers, and Deuteronomy; (2) the *Prophets,* consisting of: (*a*) the Earlier Prophets—Joshua, Judges, Samuel, and Kings—and (*b*) the Latter Prophets—Isaiah, Jeremiah, Ezekiel, and (one book) the "Twelve" or "Minor" Prophets; and (3) the *Writings,* made up of Psalms, Proverbs, Job, the Song of Songs, Ruth, Lamentations, Ecclesiastes, Esther, Daniel, Ezra (a combination of what Protestants know as Ezra and Nehemiah), and Chronicles. Terms often used are the *Pentateuch,** referring to the first five books, Genesis through Deuteronomy; the *Hexateuch,** the first six books, the Pentateuch plus Joshua;

---

* The word *Pentateuch* comes from the Greek *penta-* (meaning "five") and *teuchos* meaning "tool" or "book"). *Hexateuch* comes from the Greek *hexa-* (meaning "six") and *teuchos.*

and the "Five Rolls," or *Megilloth,* the five books from the Song of Songs through Esther.

The Roman Catholic Bible is arranged in two parts: the Old Testament and the New Testament. The Old Testament (which includes some of the books placed by Protestants in their Apocrypha) consists of forty-six books: twenty-one "historical," Genesis through Maccabees; seven "doctrinal," Job through Ecclesiasticus; and seventeen "prophetical," Isaiah through Malachi. The New Testament consists of twenty-seven books: five "historical," Matthew through Acts; twenty-one "doctrinal," Romans through Jude; and one "prophetic," Revelation, or the "Apocalypse." (Roman Catholic names of the books and spellings of the names differ in many cases from Protestant ones.)

The King James Version (as well as later Protestant versions) arranges the Bible in three parts: the Old Testament (thirty-nine books); the Apocrypha (fourteen or fifteen books—which, though not included in most modern Protestant editions, have served as useful supplements, or links, to the Old and New Testaments); and the New Testament (twenty-seven books). The arrangement of the Old Testament books differs from that of the Hebrew shown above and follows this grouping: (1) *Law* (Genesis through Deuteronomy); (2) *History* (Joshua through Esther); (3) *Poetry* (Job through the Song of Songs); (4) *Major Prophets* (Isaiah through Daniel); and (5) *Minor Prophets* (Hosea through Malachi). The books of the Apocrypha (in those editions of the King James Bible which still include them) have been placed at the end of the canonical books of the Old Testament, apparently with no effort being made toward classification. The New Testament is made up of the four *Gospels* (Matthew through John), *Acts,* twenty-one *Epistles* (Romans through Jude), and *Revelation.*

An Approach by Literary Types. Like a modern anthology of English, American, or any other literature, the Bible contains specimens of many different literary types, ranging from simple folklore to artistic lyrics and stories. In its pages we find myths, legends, fables, parables, short stories, essays, lyrics, epistles, sermons, orations, apocalypses, proverbs, history, biography, prophecy, and drama. The compilers made little attempt to arrange the writings according to the genres or according to any estimated dates of composition; consequently many different literary types, written at various times, are scattered throughout the Bible. A single book may contain several genres. Genesis, for example, is made up of myths, legends, folksongs, history, and biography. It is feasible, however, to group the books according to their dominant literary genres, and on this basis the Old Testament books treated here (selected books from Genesis through II Maccabees) are classified as "History and Biography."

ORIGIN AND EARLY TRANSMISSION OF THE BIBLE

Each of the three main divisions of Biblical literature—the Old Testament, the Apocrypha, and the New Testament—has its own unique history; hence each must be discussed as a separate unit. The chronology of the books in any one division is very difficult—and sometimes impossible—to determine. The historical and biographical books contain legends and songs which must be very ancient as well as others which must have been completed not long after the time of the events related. The prophetic books sometimes bear evidence of having originated in preaching before the Captivity, but of having been edited and annotated after the return to Jerusalem. In the New Testament the Gospel according to St. Mark was probably written before the Gospel according to St. Matthew.

The fascinating story of the writing, collecting, and canonization of the books of the Old Testament covers a period of many hundreds of years, beginning with the early stages of the Hebrew alphabet in the sixteenth and fifteenth centuries B.C.

Linguistic Difficulties for Translators. Except for five scattered passages in Aramaic, the Old Testament was written first in Hebrew. The alphabet of this language was derived from the ancient Phoenician system (North Semitic or Sinaitic). Although vowel sounds were necessarily present in *spoken* Hebrew, for hundreds of years the written alphabet consisted only of consonants. Hebrew practices applied to English would cause the first two lines of the song "America" to read as follows: MCNTRTSFTHSWTLNDFLBRT. The absence of vowels in the written language has caused much confusion among transcribers and has left the meaning of many a passage in obscurity. A given group of consonants with one set of vowels may mean one thing, whereas with another set it may mean something entirely different. For example, the Hebrew letters which correspond to $S - PH - R$ may be read "to count," "to declare," "a scribe," or a "book."[2] Further difficulty in the reading of ancient Hebrew has been caused by the forbidding of ligatures (regarded as desecrations of the holy text) in Scriptural writings, by the similarity of some Hebrew letters, and by the lack of spacing between words and even between prose sentences or lines of poetry. Thus, although the Hebrew scribes often took the utmost pains to transcribe the Scriptures accurately, misunderstandings arose.

The primitive Hebrew language was a member of the Semitic family; it was similar to—and apparently derived from—ancient Chaldean (Babylonian) and Phoenician languages. The numerous invasions, defeats, and periods of captivity suffered by the Hebrews resulted in the mingling of many foreign elements with their primitive speech. This altered language became known as "Aramaic," and by 300 B.C. it had almost entirely supplanted Hebrew as the spoken language of the Hebrews.

In view of the fact that the Old Testament was originally written in Hebrew, it is a surprising fact, that, except for the Pentateuch, most of the book of Isaiah (found in one of the famous Dead Sea [Qumran] scrolls), and brief fragments of other books, no Hebrew manuscript of the Old Testament now available can be assigned to a date earlier than the ninth century A.D. Medieval as well as modern editors and translators have had to rely chiefly on Greek and other versions rather than on Hebrew manuscripts of the Old Testament as their most ancient sources.

Composition, Collection, and Canonization. The belief that the Hebrew alphabet was in existence as early as the sixteenth century B.C. would indicate the possibility of a written literature of that period. It is doubtful, however, that any actual writings have been preserved from such an early date. The oldest fragments of the Old Testament may date as far back as the wanderings in the Wilderness (at some time between 1400 and 1200 B.C.) or even earlier, but as something remembered and transmitted orally before being preserved in written form. It seems almost certain that by the middle of the tenth century a scribe or scribes were writing the history of David's kingdom. The latest of the Old Testament writings (if those of the Apocrypha are excluded)—Ecclesiastes, Daniel, and Esther—were probably written during the second century B.C.

It is not known who first collected into one volume the diverse literary writings that now make up the Old Testament. It is believed that the Law was "canonized" (accepted as divinely inspired and divinely authorized) between 450 and 350 B.C. For the Hebrews in the time of Jesus and the Apostles, the Law was the most authoritative division of the Scriptures. Next in degree of inspiration and authority came the Prophets. It is believed that these eight books (the Twelve Minor Prophets having been lumped together as a single "book") were canonized about 200 B.C. Least in authority, and perhaps for that reason the last to be canonized (in the second century B.C.), were the Writings. The Old Testament also refers to several books no longer extant which may at one time have been regarded by the Hebrews as Holy Scripture. (Note references to "Chronicles of the Kings of Israel" in I Kings 14:19 *et seq.* and to "Chronicles of the Kings of Judah" in I Kings 14:29 *et seq.*)

The Hebrew Scriptures (Masoretic Text). There are many reasons for the almost total lack of early Hebrew texts. In the first place, the wars and persecutions which the Hebrews suffered must have destroyed a great deal of their literature. Possibly the three greatest disasters for the Old Testament were the destruction of Jerusalem by Nebuchadrezzar in 586 B.C.; the attempt by Antiochus Epiphanes in 168 B.C. to wipe out all Hebrew culture and religion; and the destruction of Jerusalem by the Romans in A.D. 70. No doubt many ancient Hebrew manuscripts were destroyed deliberately by scribes who wanted to prevent worn-out copies from falling into impious hands or who wanted to prevent what they considered errors from being perpetuated.

From about A.D. 600 to 925, groups of scribes and textual critics known as the "Masoretes" were given the responsibility of preserving and transmitting the traditional Hebrew text of the Scriptures. They carried on their activities in several regions, including Mesopotamia, Babylonia, and Palestine. They derived their name from the Hebrew word *masoreth* (meaning "tradition"), which was applied to the vast number of marginal notes and notes at the ends of the Biblical books. These notes contained, among other matters, variant readings and directions for pronunciation. Perhaps the most extraordinary contribution—and certainly one of the most valuable—was an invention by the Masoretes of a system of vowel sounds and accentual marks, which they inserted into the traditional texts made up of consonants alone. The Masoretes were devoted and painstaking scholars, and it is on their texts that Hebrew Bibles are based today.

Another important Hebrew version of part of the Old Testament was the work of the Samaritans, the inhabitants of the region around the city of Samaria after the Hebrews' return from Exile. Recognizing only the Pentateuch as Holy Scripture, in the fourth century B.C. the Samaritans made their own copies of the first five books of the Old Testament. Since the Samaritans spoke Hebrew, the Samaritan Pentateuch is exceedingly valuable as an independent Hebrew text, preserved by a tradition entirely outside of the Masoretic one.

The Greek Old Testament (The Septuagint). After the conquests of Alexander the Great, the Hellenization of the Mediterranean lands was rapid and rather thorough. The Greek language quickly gained a foothold in Asia Minor and North Africa. By the middle of the third century B.C., there was a distinct need for a Greek translation of the Holy Scriptures because many Egyptian Jews who remained loyal to their ancient faith had adopted the Greek tongue.

The circumstances surrounding the Greek translation have been subject to controversy. An old tradition holds that Ptolemy Philadelphus (who reigned 285-246 B.C.) requested the high priest in Jerusalem to send him a group of scholars who would translate the Law into Greek for his library. The priest obliged and sent Ptolemy seventy-two scholars, who in exactly seventy-two days completed the translation of the Pentateuch. Another version of this story tells that the seventy-two scholars broke up into pairs, that each pair, working separately, translated the whole Law, and that, after the work had been completed, the thirty-six copies were found to be identical! To some scholars it seems more likely that, in contrast to these legends, the Jews in Alexandria were themselves responsible for having the translation made in order to serve those who knew Greek better than Hebrew. The name *Septuagint* (frequently abbreviated as *LXX*), which is applied to this Greek version of the Old Testament, is derived from the Latin word for *seventy*, and it is generally supposed that it refers to the number of translators. Another conjecture is that the name was used for this translation because there were seventy members of the Alexandrian Sanhedrin (Jewish council and tribunal).

Although the facts about the translating are unknown, most scholars agree that the Pentateuch was rendered into Greek in Alexandria about the middle of the third century B.C. The remaining parts of the Old Testament were translated by different scholars at various times during the next century and a half; it is thought that the whole was probably completed about 100 B.C. Naturally enough, the quality of the different books is uneven. Some of the books are quite literally rendered, others freely. Some of the translators took great liberties with the Hebrew text, changing, omitting, or inserting words or phrases as they thought best. It is almost certain that some of the scholars had sources which are not available to us today.

Abandoning in part the traditional Hebrew order and adding the books which now constitute the Protestant Apocrypha, the Septuagint helped establish the order of the books followed in general by most Christian Bibles before the Reformation.

The Greek manuscripts are of two types: uncials and cursives. An uncial (from Latin uncialis, meaning "an inch high") is written in large, separate letters; a cursive is written in a smaller, "running" hand, as the name implies. Most of the uncials, about thirty of which survive, date from the third to the tenth century A.D. The cursives are generally later—from the ninth to the sixteenth century—but some are much older (a few fragments are perhaps from the second century B.C.). More than fifteen hundred cursive manuscripts are known to exist.

The most important uncial manuscripts are the *Codex* Vaticanus (B), A.D. 300-350; the *Codex Sinaiticus* (S), c. A.D. 350; the *Codex Alexandrinus* (A) c. A.D. 400-450); and the *Codex Ephraemi* (C), c. A.D. 400-500.

The Septuagint was the version of the Old Testament known to the early Christians, who quoted from it to prove that Jesus had fulfilled the old prophecies and was therefore the promised Messiah. So persuasive were their arguments that eventually many of the Hebrews who adhered to Judaism began to consider the

---

* A *codex* is a book made up of manuscript pages bound together in a way similar to that in use today—as distinguished from a "roll" or "scroll."

Septuagint a Christian Bible and to lose faith in it as a trustworthy rendering of their ancient Hebrew Scriptures. Consequently several "rival" translations appeared in the early Christian centuries.

The great age of our extant copies of the Septuagint and the
early dates of its rivals and revisions virtually require all serious
students of the Bible to study it.

**The Latin Old Testament ("Old Latin" Versions* and the
Vulgate).** It appears that both Hebrews and Christians felt a
need for a Latin version of the Holy Scriptures and that by A.D.
200 the whole of the Old Testament had been translated piecemeal into that language.

Equal in importance to the Septuagint was the Latin translation of the Old Testament made by St. Jerome (Eusebius Hier-
onymus, c. 340-420), who revised the Old Latin Scriptures on   *Vulgate*
the basis of the Hebrew and Greek texts. He did not attempt a
strictly word-for-word translation, but preferred to employ idiomatic language. His free translation, which was very graceful and
readable, came to be called the Vulgate, or "People's" version.
(A revision of his text was made by the English scholar Alcuin
in the eighth century as directed by Charlemagne.)

The Vulgate did not immediately supplant the Old Latin versions; and, indeed, it met with much opposition on the part of
conservatives who clung to the earlier and more traditional versions. By the seventh century, however, the Vulgate and the Old
Latin versions were used about equally, and the Vulgate thereafter steadily gained in popularity. During the remainder of the
Middle Ages the latter was *the* version for the Western Christian
nations and still is, for the Roman Catholic Church, the authoritative standard for use in liturgy, pulpit, and theological discussions.

Syriac and Aramaic Versions (Peshitta and Targums). The Hebrew, Greek, and Latin versions of the Old Testament are, of
course, by far the most important ones. Nevertheless, there are
many others—some of great antiquity—which scholars have found
to be helpful in their attempts to determine the "original" reading
of many passages. Two of the most significant of these versions are the *Peshitta* (or *Peshitto*) and the *Targums*. The Peshitta is the Syriac (or East Aramaic) version of the Old Testa-

* A term applied to pre-Vulgate versions of the Bible.

Peshitta
(syriac)

Targums
(Aramaic)

ment, which is helpful to Biblical scholars because it is an early, independent translation from the Hebrew (one extant manuscript of part of the Pentateuch dates from the fifth century A.D., and a manuscript of the whole of the Old Testament, from the sixth century). The value of the Peshitta as an independent text is reduced by the fact that some of its revisions were made to agree with Septuagintal readings. The Targums are Aramaic translations of the Hebrew text, plus a large amount of paraphrase and explanatory matter. Originally used in synagogues in Aramaic lands, the Targums were for a long time transmitted orally. The first mention of written Targums belongs to the first century A.D., although it is possible that some were put into writing before the Christian era. Most of the extant Targums are from the fifth century A.D. or later. They are of minor importance in textual criticism, but they throw a considerable amount of light on ancient Hebrew tradition and exegesis.

The Apocrypha. The term *Apocrypha** is now generally employed to designate fourteen or fifteen books which were included in the Septuagint or the Vulgate but which were not considered by the Palestinian Jews to have been genuinely inspired and which were not then extant in the original Hebrew. The Apocryphal books are as follows: Tobit, Judith, The Rest of Esther, The Wisdom of Solomon, Ecclesiasticus (the Wisdom of Jesus, son of Sirach), Baruch (with the Epistle of Jeremiah, sometimes printed as a separate book), The Song of the Three Children, Susanna and the Elders, Bel and the Dragon, I and II Maccabees, I and II Esdras, and The Prayer of Manasses.

The early Christians considered all the books of the Septuagint as more or less canonical. When preparing the Vulgate, St. Jerome returned to the Hebrew text as his guide; he included all the Septuagintal books, but labeled those not in the Hebrew

* A plural derived from Greek *apokryphos,* meaning "hidden" or "supplementary" or "spurious." In addition to these books attached to the Old Testament, there are many others (termed *Pseudepigrapha,* meaning "falsely inscribed") which were usually ascribed to well-known Jewish authors. They were written between 200 B.C. and A.D. 200 in Hebrew, Aramaic, or Greek; and they include a variety of genres: legends, psalms, gospels, apocalypses, history, and popular philosophy. See Robert H. Pfeiffer, "The Literature and Religion of the Pseudepigrapha," *The Interpreter's Bible,* I, 421-436.

canon as Apocryphal); and he added three more (also listed as Apocryphal) and placed them after the book of Revelation in the New Testament); these three were The Prayer of Manasses and III and IV Esdras.*

During the Reformation the Protestant churches adopted as canonical only those books which had been in the Hebrew canon. The Roman Catholic Church, on the contrary, accepted as canonical all the books in the Septuagint except III and IV Maccabees, and it rejected St. Jerome's Prayer of Manasses and III and IV Esdras. The Church of England accepted fourteen books of the Protestant Apocrypha for purposes of edification rather than "for the establishment of doctrine." In the Coverdale Bible (1535) and in the King James version (1611) these books were separated from the canonical ones and placed between the Old Testament and the New Testament. From a literary point of view it is regrettable that these books have been omitted from most contemporary Protestant Bibles.

The New Testament. The history of the writing and transmission of the New Testament is far simpler than that of the Old Testament. The languages in which it was first written are less confusing than the ancient Hebrew; the dates of composition, collection, and canonization have been approximated; and the extant manuscripts are closer in time to the dates of their original composition than are those of the Old Testament. Many grammatical constructions and idioms in certain portions (Gospels and Acts) may indicate a possible Aramaic version, but no such

---

* The Protestant Bible divides the single book Ezra of the old Hebrew canon into two books, Ezra and Nehemiah.

The Septuagint Bible made up the book Esdras by reworking the Hebrew book Ezra and adding part of what is now II Chronicles in the Protestant Bible. It also repeated the same Hebrew book Ezra as II Esdras.

The Vulgate Bible added a legend in Josephus to the Septuagintal I Esdras to constitute the book III Esdras. The Vulgate IV Esdras (called II Esdras in the King James Version) is an apocalyptic book; it is called III Esdras when Ezra and Nehemiah are combined in one book. Thus, in the Protestant Apocrypha, I Esdras is approximately the same as the Septuagintal I Esdras, while II Esdras is approximately the same as the Vulgate IV Esdras.

The Roman Catholic (Douay) version includes I and II Esdras as canonical books corresponding, respectively, to the Protestant Ezra and Nehemiah.

version has been discovered, and Biblical scholars now treat the Greek text as if it were the original. The various epistles and the book of Revelation were almost certainly written first in Greek. All the canonical books of the New Testament were probably written within a century following the death of Jesus—most of them between A.D. 64 and 105. There are several thousand known manuscripts of the Greek New Testament. The Latin-speaking Christians possessed translations from the Greek Scriptures as early as the second century—perhaps during the first. About fifty Old Latin manuscripts survive. Much of what has been said above about the Latin Old Testament is applicable also to the Latin New Testament.

THE ENGLISH BIBLE BEFORE 1611

There has never been—and there probably never will be—a really definitive English translation of the Bible, for new translations will be needed as long as archeological, linguistic, and historical discoveries continue to throw new light on the Scriptures. This point has been strikingly illustrated during the past decade as the study of the Dead Sea Scrolls has suggested some new conjectures and interpretations subsequent to publication (1946, 1952) of the superb Revised Standard Version.

During the past five centuries dozens of English translations have been made. Some of these, though of great historical and scholarly significance, are no longer in common use and therefore are of relatively minor concern to the student of the Bible as literature. Several modern versions have considerable literary interest and value, however—some because they are eloquent and poetic, others because they are literal.

The Bible entered England at the end of the sixth century A.D. In 597 the monk Augustine came to that island as a Christian missionary, bringing with him from Rome nine books (all in Latin, of course): a two-volume copy of the Bible, two Psalters, two copies of the Gospels, and three other religious books.[3] These were England's first library.

Knowledge of Biblical subject matter was spread orally, and within less than a century vernacular works on Biblical themes were appearing. Then came translations in Old and Middle English, leading in the sixteenth century to various Protestant Bibles and an official Roman Catholic Bible.

Old and Middle English Paraphrases and Translations (*c.* 670-1380). Many paraphrases, interlinear glosses, and translations of parts of the Latin Bible appeared between 670 and 1380. The majority of these were intended for use by the clergy, only a few being for popular reading. The Psalms and the Gospels were the favorite books.

Wyclifite Bibles (*c.* 1380-82). Near the end of the fourteenth century John Wyclif (*c.* 1320-84) and his assistants produced *the first complete Bible in English*. It is not known how much of the translation Wyclif himself did, but he was the inspirational force behind the project; it is believed that Nicholas of Hereford, one of his followers, translated most of the Old Testament. The New Testament was finished about 1380; the Old Testament, about 1382. This "Wyclif-Hereford" version was a translation of the Vulgate. Even in its own day it was not an entirely satisfactory translation; it followed slavishly the word order of St. Jerome's Latin, and the style was often stilted and somewhat crude. A revision, completed before the end of the century and attributed to one John Purvey, attempted successfully to establish a more authentic text and to make the language more up-to-date and idiomatic. The "Lollards," as Wyclif's disciples were called, must have produced astounding numbers of manuscript copies, for more than 170 have survived to the present day.

The Tyndale Bible (*c.* 1525-34). During the third and fourth decades of the sixteenth century William Tyndale (*c.* 1492-1536), using the best available Hebrew, Greek, and Latin texts, produced an English version of the New Testament, of the Old Testament from Genesis through Chronicles, of Jonah, and of parts of the Apocrypha. The English-speaking world is indebted to Tyndale for several contributions: (1) *his New Testament was the first part of the Bible to be printed in English* (1525 or 1526); (2) *he was the first to attempt a genuinely scholarly translation of the Bible from its original languages into English;* and (3) because of its influence on later translators, *his work can be considered a landmark in the development of English prose style.* (His revised New Testament of 1534 has been the basis for subsequent versions down to our own times.)

The Versions of George Joye (1530-c. 1535). George Joye, at one time an associate of Tyndale, gave us the first printed English versions of the Psalms (1530, revised 1534), Isaiah (1531), Jeremiah and Lamentations (1534), and perhaps Proverbs and Ecclesiastes (c. 1535). Although much of his translation was very free and some of his diction infelicitous, his work appreciably influenced later translations.

The Coverdale Bible (1535). In 1535 Miles Coverdale (1488?-1569) produced *the first complete Bible printed in English*. More an editor than an original translator, Coverdale made no attempt to find the earliest and most "authentic" texts; but he did gather the best sources with which he himself could deal competently, and he tried to harmonize them. The English-speaking world owes him a debt of gratitude for (1) numerous beautiful and felicitous phrases, copied and preserved in later translations, and (2) the first printed version of the English Apocrypha as a whole and a large portion of the Old Testament—Esther, Job, and all the prophets from Ezekiel through Malachi.

The Matthew Bible (1537). A version of the Scriptures now known as the "Matthew Bible" appeared in 1537. Its title-page describes it as a new translation by one Thomas Matthew; actually it is a compilation (chiefly of Tyndale and Coverdale texts), and the compiler is believed to have been John Rogers, a Protestant who for political reasons wished to keep his name secret. Its only important contribution was the printing of the hitherto-unpublished translation of the so-called "historical" books (Joshua through II Chronicles) attributed to Tyndale.

The Taverner Bible (1539). In 1539 Richard Taverner revised the Matthew Bible, making a considerable number of verbal changes based on his expert knowledge of Greek. This version was of relatively small importance, but occasionally it hit upon a fortunate phrase preserved in later Bibles.

The Great Bible (1539-41). As late as 1539 no Bible had been royally authorized in England. Now, Thomas Cromwell, Henry VIII's most influential minister, and Thomas Cranmer, Archbishop of Canterbury, desired an English translation which the whole nation would find acceptable. Cromwell chose Coverdale to supervise the project. The first edition came from the press in 1539. The format of the first printing was a large folio; hence the name "the Great Bible" was given to the version. A second printing appeared in the following year. These two issues of the first edition are sometimes called "Cromwell's Bible." To the second through the fifth editions (1540-41) was added a long preface by Archbishop Cranmer. All these editions are referred to as "Cranmer's Bible."

Although Coverdale made some use of Hebrew, Latin, and Greek texts, this version was essentially a revision of the Matthew Bible supplemented by portions of the Old Testament (e.g., Ezekiel through Malachi) and of the Apocrypha based on Coverdale's 1535 version.

An injunction by Cromwell and subsequent injunctions by Henry VIII firmly established the Great Bible over a long period as *the* Bible for English-speaking people. The Psalter for the Anglican Book of Common Prayer was adopted from the Great Bible and still remains in use with little alteration.

The Geneva Bible (1557, 1560). Mary Tudor's persecution of Protestants caused many to flee to the Continent. Some, along with other political and religious refugees from all over Europe, sought haven in Geneva, Switzerland. One group, including John Calvin, John Knox, Miles Coverdale, and Theodore Beza (the foremost Biblical scholar of the time) undertook a new English translation of the Bible. In 1557 they published at Geneva their version of the New Testament; the whole Bible, exclusive of the Apocrypha, appeared three years later.

The Geneva Bible was a thorough revision based on the Great Bible version of the Old Testament and on a 1552 edition of Tyndale's New Testament. The translators (or revisers) also used various Greek and Latin texts.

The Geneva Bible introduced many innovations. It was the first English Bible: (1) to be printed in roman instead of black-letter type; (2) to divide the text into verses;* (3) to use italic print for words which were not in the original languages but which the translators felt needed to be added for the sake of clarity. It was printed in quarto form, and so because of its relatively small size and its legibility it was far more convenient than the black-letter folio of the Great Bible. It contained a preface by Calvin and marginal notes of distinctly Calvinistic

---

* For the division of the Bible into chapters, we are indebted to the *Sacrorum Bibliorum Concordantiae* of Cardinal Hugo of Saneto Caro (*c.* 1200-1263).

and Puritan bias. Furthermore, it provided tables, maps, woodcuts, chapter summaries, running titles, and (after 1579) a Calvinistic catechism.[4]

The translation itself was the best that had been made up to that time. In the first place, the scholarship which produced it was more thorough than that behind any previous edition. The translators aimed at such a literal rendering that they felt it necessary to apologize (in the preface) for the preservation of the "Ebrewe phrases" that might sound harsh to readers familiar with other versions. It is true that this striving for accuracy sometimes made the diction bare and unpoetic, but most of it was lofty and forceful, and its simplicity appealed to the average reader. Innumerable passages were taken over word for word by the King James translators.

Despite its dedication to Queen Elizabeth, the Geneva Bible never became the official or authorized version for the English Church; the Calvinistic notes probably prevented its adoption. But it became so popular that at least 140 editions were published between 1560 and 1644, and before 1611 (date of publication of the King James Bible) it was probably read by more people than any other English version. Although it has been called "the Bible of Shakespeare, of John Bunyan, of Cromwell's army, of the Puritan pilgrims, and of King James himself," [5] there is some doubt about which version of the Bible Shakespeare and Bunyan used.

The Bishops' Bible (1568). Royal and ecclesiastical disapproval of the Calvinistic tendencies of the Geneva Bible led to the decision that another English version was needed. In 1566 Matthew Parker, Archbishop of Canterbury, was chosen as editor-in-chief. He divided the actual task of revision and annotation among a group of bishops and other church scholars. Some of these did little more than copy out the text of the Great Bible; some tried to blend the Geneva and the Great Bible texts; still others made sweeping changes of their own. The result was a Bible sadly lacking in uniformity. The book of Psalms was so bad that in the fourth and all later editions (except one of 1585) the version found in the Great Bible was substituted.

Inferior though it was, the Bishops' Bible, by order of the Archbishop, supplanted the Great Bible—at least in church services. Only one edition of the latter was published (1569) after Parker's Bible appeared. Outside the Church the Bishops' Bible was never so popular as the Geneva Bible, but the demand was sufficiently great to warrant the publication of twenty editions, the last appearing in 1606.

In only a few instances did the King James Version follow the Bishops' Bible.

The Rheims-Douay Bible (1582-1609). Just as the Protestants fled from England during the reign of Queen Mary, so the Catholics exiled themselves to escape persecution by Queen Elizabeth. Many Catholic exiles settled at Douai in Flanders, some of them moving later to Rheims. A group of them, under the leadership of Gregory Martin, undertook to produce an English version of the Bible which would be acceptable to Romanists. The New Testament was published at Rheims in 1582 and hence is known as the "Rheims New Testament"; subsequently it became part of the so-called "Douay Bible." It was not till 1609-10 that the Old Testament translation was published at Douai.

The title page stated that the translation was made from the "authentical Latin"—that is, from the Vulgate—and that editions in Greek and "other" languages were consulted.

The Douai translators, fearing that they might change the sense of the "divinely inspired" Vulgate version, tried to translate the Latin as literally as possible and therefore did not achieve the eloquence later to be found in the freer and more idiomatic King James Version; it should be remembered, however, that for scholarly purposes, there is still a good deal of value in literal translations.

The Rheims-Douay Bible is significant (1) because it is the basis of modern Roman Catholic English Bibles (see p. 36, below) and (2) because it exerted an appreciable influence on the diction of the King James Version.[6]

MODERN VERSIONS OF THE ENGLISH BIBLE

There are several versions of the Bible now in use in the churches and the homes of English-speaking people all over the world. Each has its own particular merits and shortcomings; all are worthy of the respect and attention of students of literature.

Some adhere rather closely to certain traditions; others are more willing to accept and incorporate the conclusions of the "higher criticism" and of modern science. Some are fairly literal renderings of ancient manuscripts; others are comparatively free translations. Some are valued for their eloquence, others for their simplicity and clarity. Some retain the centuries-old tradition of printing all the Bible as prose and observing merely the chapter-and-verse conventions within each book; others attempt to appeal to the modern reader by dividing prose passages into logical paragraphs and by printing poetry *as* poetry—that is, by preserving the integrity of each line of verse and beginning each line with a capital letter. The table on pages 34-35 may prove useful for comparison of seven versions most widely used today.

The King James Bible (1611). When James I acceded to the throne in 1603, there were three Bibles in use in England: the Bishops' Bible, which was used in most churches; the Great Bible, which was still used in some rural churches; and the Geneva Bible, which was found in many homes. None of these was entirely satisfactory. The Bishops' Bible was an uneven production which had never pleased either scholars or the people in general; the Great Bible was cumbersome and hard to read; and the Geneva Bible smacked of Puritanism.

Aware of the widespread use of all three versions, King James felt that one official version would not only help bind his nation together and lessen theological disputes, but also be a credit to his regime. In 1604 he appointed fifty-four * learned men to make a new translation. Apparently they were selected solely on their merits as Biblical scholars and not on the basis of their religious leanings, for some were Anglican churchmen, some were Puritans, and some were laymen. They were divided into six groups—two each at Oxford, Cambridge, and Westminster. Each group revised a specific portion of the Scriptures; their revision was finally edited by a committee of six. The new version was completed in 1610 and published in 1611.

The first King James Bible was a folio volume, printed in black-letter type; roman type was used for words supplied by the

---

* The extant list contains only the names of the forty-seven men who actually served.

revisers but not in the original Hebrew, Aramaic, or Greek.* The Apocrypha was placed between the two Testaments. Included were a preface, a table of contents, an almanac, various tables, and (in some copies) a map of Canaan and a genealogical chart. At the beginning of each chapter there was a summary of its contents.

This version was as accurate a translation as early seventeenth-century scholarship could achieve. The scholars appointed by the king made a conscientious effort to avail themselves of the most trustworthy texts and commentaries—"Chaldee, Hebrewe, Syrian, Greeke . . . , Latin, Spanish, French, Italian . . . [and] Dutch." Apparently they made use, too, of all the previously printed English versions. Except in interpolated chapter synopses, they tried not to go counter to their sources or beyond them. If they were obliged for the sake of clarity to supply English words, they indicated this typographically (by roman type, as mentioned above). It must be remembered, however, that compared with mid-twentieth-century scholars who have access to numerous manuscript sources and photostats and who know more about ancient history, ancient linguistics, and ancient prosody, the King James translators were at a great disadvantage.

They were not only conscientious scholars but also excellent literary stylists. They were fortunate in that the English language during Jacobean times was perhaps closer to the Hebrew and Greek than it has been since. The translators did an almost miraculous job of choosing effective wording, whether derived from an earlier English version or originated by the King James scholars themselves.[7] They deliberately used various synonyms for the translation of a single Hebrew or Greek word for the sake of variety and richness. An amazing merit of the 1611 Bible is the uniformity of diction and style. Its homogeneity and evenness make it impossible for a reader without inside information to ascertain where one scholar or company of scholars began or left off. The genius with which they made use of their materials has been the subject of many articles and whole books. Perhaps it is sufficient to say here that—despite the passage of centuries

* Modern editions (1) are printed in roman type, with the revisers' interpolations in italics, and (2) have been modernized in spelling and given minor revisions.

COMPARISON OF MODERN BIBLES

Characteristics	King James	Modern Douay (1950)	English Revised and American Standard
Tradition Followed	Follows Tyndale tradition. Borrows from most of the other 16th-century Bibles.	Faithful to Roman Catholic tradition. Follows Douay version of 1750, which is a revision of the Rheims-Douay Bible of 1582-1609.	Faithful to English and American Protestant tradition. Uses King James Version as basis, but adopts many conclusions of "higher criticism" and of science.
Literalness of Translation	Fairly free translation.	Literal, conservative translation of Vulgate.	Idiomatic, but very literal translation.
Style and Diction	Eloquent, colorful, fluent. Some of Jacobean diction now obsolete.	Latinistic, but limited modernization of diction.	Simple, and clear. Some of diction is modernized, but many archaic forms retained. English Revised Version employs British locutions; American Standard, American locutions.
Mechanics, Spelling, and Punctuation	Uses traditional chapter-and-verse divisions only.	Psalms (Confraternity text) indicates poetry typographically; other books use only chapter-and-verse divisions, with no attempt at paragraphing and no distinction between prose and verse.	Chapter-and-verse markings retained, but prose is divided into paragraphs. Some (but not all) poetry indicated typographically.

COMPARISON OF MODERN BIBLES (CONT.)

Moffatt	Hebrew (1917)	Smith-Goodspeed	Revised Standard
Abandons King James tradition.	Adheres to Masoretic tradition.	Abandons most church traditions; utilizes all available data from science and "higher criticism."	Follows King James tradition, but makes many changes on basis of 20th-century discoveries in archaeology, linguistics, etc.
Exceptionally free translation—sometimes almost a paraphrase.	Fairly free translation of Masoretic text.	Fairly free.	Idiomatic but literal translation.
Simple, conversational. Modernized diction; uses *thou*, *thy*, etc., only for Deity.	Eloquent, fluent. Adopts many of King James readings, but modernizes some of diction. Retains *thou* forms.	Aims at simplicity and current American usage. Modernizes verb endings, uses *thou* forms only for Deity.	Retains some of King James eloquence, but simplifies and modernizes the diction. Modernizes verb endings; uses *thou* forms only for Deity.
Chapter-and-verse markings retained. Modernizes spelling, punctuation, and mechanics. Prose divided into paragraphs. Poetry indicated typographically.	Retains chapter-and-verse markings. Indicates poetry typographically. Divides prose into paragraphs.	Places chapter-and-verse markings in margin. Indicates poetry typographically. Divides prose into paragraphs.	Retains chapter-and-verse markings. Indicates poetry typographically. Divides prose into paragraphs. Places variant or rejected passages in footnotes.

and the publication of such modern Bibles as the Smith-Good-speed translation and the Revised Standard Version—the King James Bible, judged merely as a piece of literature, is still considered by many to be the finest English version of the Scriptures.*

For the modern student the principal shortcomings of the King James Bible are (1) occasional inaccuracy of translation, (2) obscurity resulting from the use of words which are now archaic or obsolete, and (3) failure to distinguish typographically between poetry and prose.[8] Anyone who wishes to understand the King James Version thoroughly needs to read a modern-speech translation concurrently and to consult a commentary.

Modern Roman Catholic Bibles. In 1750 and again in 1763 Bishop Richard Challoner of London and Francis Blyth—both converts to Catholicism—made a major revision of the Rheims-Douay Old Testament. (Challoner completed several revisions of the Rheims-Douay New Testament, the last in 1772). Influenced considerably by the King James Bible, Challoner greatly improved the syntax and diction of the 1609 Catholic version, especially by weeding out many archaisms and Latinistic constructions. The Challoner text (though subsequently revised several times) has remained "the standard English Catholic Bible";[9] a recent revision has been undertaken by The Episcopal Committee of the Confraternity of Christian Doctrine; the New Testament appeared in 1941, Genesis in 1948, the Psalms and Canticles (Song of Songs) in 1950, and Exodus through Ruth in 1956; some of the remaining books of the Old Testament are still in preparation.

There are two other notable Catholic versions of the twentieth century: (1) the Westminster Bible, edited by Cuthbert Lattey and Joseph Keating, an independent translation from the Hebrew and Greek, published piecemeal between 1913 and 1935 and in a single-volume edition in 1948; (2) the Knox Bible, translated by Ronald A. Knox, not a revision of the Challoner text,

---

* This Outline will use the King James Version as a basis for discussion and for all references and quotations unless some other version is specified.

Although called the "Authorized Version," the King James Bible was never officially "authorized" by either king or Parliament. The king's appointment of the fifty-four scholars was the only authorization that took place.

but a *new translation of the Vulgate*, with cognizance being taken of Hebrew and Greek sources (the New Testament appeared in 1944, part of the Old Testament in 1948, and the remainder in 1950).

The Revised Version and the American Standard Version (1881-1901). The King James Bible was so generally acceptable that no Protestant ecclesiastical body made any official attempt to bring about a major revision till late in the nineteenth century. By that time many archaeological and linguistic discoveries and many changes in the English language since 1611 warranted a new revision. In 1870, at the invitation of the Convocation of the Anglican Church, fifty-two British scholars undertook the task. The New Testament was published in 1881, the Old and New Testament in one volume in 1885, and the Apocrypha separately in 1895. This was called the Revised Version or the English Revised Version.

Although the revisers adopted many conclusions of contemporary scientists and of the "higher critics," they were faithful to English Protestant tradition, and they endeavored to alter the King James text *only* when "faithfulness" to the best obtainable source material so dictated. They modernized punctuation and mechanics; they relegated chapter-and-verse numerals to the margins; they distinguished some (but not all) of the poetical passages from prose typographically; and they indicated the logical divisions of prose passages by paragraphing. They tried to give idiomatic expression to a literal rendering of their sources. They aimed rather at accuracy, simplicity, and clarity than at eloquence and magnificence. Unlike the King James translators, they strove for consistency in the translation of each Hebrew and Greek word. They modernized some of the Jacobean diction of the King James Version, but retained such archaisms as the *-eth* and *-edst* forms of verbs (*thirsteth, walkedst*) and the "familiar" second-person-singular pronouns *thee, thou, thy, thine.*

A group of thirty American Biblical scholars was invited to co-operate with the British revisers. It was agreed that the American company would send its suggestions to the British committee before final decisions were made, and the English revisers were to adopt whatever suggestions they thought wise and to include all others in an appendix. The American group agreed not to give their support to the publication of any other edition for fourteen years after the appearance of the English Revised Version.

The inclusion of many antiquated words (such as *holpen* for *helped*) and a number of others which passed currency in Great Britain but not in the United States (such as *corn* for *grain*) induced the American company to bring out its own edition in 1901. This edition contained an appendix listing the readings of the English Revised Version which the American scholars had rejected.* The title page of the American volume was the same as that for the British except that there was added: "Newly Edited by the American Revision Committee. A.D. 1901. Standard Edition." Hence it has come to be called the "American Standard Version."

Moffatt's Translation (1913, 1924). James Moffatt published a modern-speech translation of the New Testament in 1913 and of the Old Testament in 1924; both Testaments were published together in one volume in 1926. Believing the Hebrew text to be "often desperately corrupt," he undertook to correct it by (1) amending phrases which he found "broken or defective," (2) shifting "phrases . . . , verses, and sometimes . . . entire sections," and (3) inserting words or phrases he regarded as necessary.[10] This version is not merely a revision but a completely new translation—a translation so free and in such modern, colloquial language that I. M. Price has called it "often a paraphrase rather than a translation" and "Moffatt's running commentary on the whole Bible." [11] It uses the *thou* forms of the pronoun only in reference to the Deity; it abandons the archaic verb forms; it indicates poetic passages typographically; and it divides prose into logical paragraphs—retaining, however, the traditional chapter-and-verse numerals. Though an exceptionally free translation, it is an interesting and enlightening version.

The Hebrew Scriptures (1917). A number of times during the last two centuries, Jewish scholars have revised their English translation of the Holy Scriptures.[12] The most noteworthy version is one published in 1917 by the Jewish Publication Society of America. The revisers spent some twenty-five years consulting not only the Masoretic text, on which the revision is based, but

---

* Many critics have considered one change made by the Americans to be especially undesirable: the rendering of the Hebrew *YHVH* as "Jehovah" instead of "the Lord."

also many other significant ancient versions (Septuagint, Vulgate, Targums, Peshitta, and others) and all existing English Bibles.[13] In style and diction it is similar to the King James Version; it employs the archaic verb endings and "familiar" pronominal forms. It distinguishes typographically between poetry and prose. This version of the Hebrew Scriptures was reprinted, with minor revisions, in 1955. (A new translation of the Pentateuch, introducing modern interpretations of the original Hebrew was published by the Jewish Publication Society in 1963.)

The Smith-Goodspeed Translation, The "Chicago Bible" (1923-39). A valuable and attractive translation of the Bible was made during the third and fourth decades of this century. In 1923 E. J. Goodspeed brought out his version of the New Testament. Four years later J. M. P. Smith, A. R. Gordon, T. J. Meek, and Leroy Waterman published their translation of the Old Testament. In 1931 the Old Testament of Smith *et al.* and the New Testament of Goodspeed were combined in a single volume, entitled *The Bible—An American Translation.* In 1938 Goodspeed translated and published the Apocrypha, and in 1939 this was included with the two Testaments in *The Complete Bible: An American Translation.* This and the 1931 edition are often called the "Chicago Bible."

This was a fairly free translation which modernized and Americanized the diction. The term "the Lord" was used in place of "Jehovah" (which was used in the American Standard Version); the forms *thou, thee,* etc., were used only in reference to the Deity; and special typographical means were used to distinguish verse from prose.

The Revised Standard Version (1946-57). A period of forty-five years was to elapse between the appearance of the American Standard Version and that of the next "authorized" version of the Bible. During that time many ancient papyri in Koiné had been discovered, and therefore much progress had been made in understanding Biblical Greek. Furthermore, the modern-speech versions (such as the Smith-Goodspeed) and the free translations (such as that of Moffatt) had called much popular attention to the infelicities in the diction of the Revised and the American Standard versions.

In 1929 the International Council of Religious Education, representing forty Protestant denominations in the United States and

Canada, set in motion the machinery for the preparation of a new revision. Thirty-two scholars participated. The New Testament was finished first and published separately in 1946. The Old Testament was completed in 1951, and both Testaments were published in a single volume in 1952. The Revised Standard Version of the Apocrypha was published in 1957.

Using the American Standard Version as their point of departure, the revisers consulted all the best obtainable sources. The diction was brought up to date. The -eth and -edst forms of the verbs were abandoned; and *thou, thee, thy,* and *thine* were used only to refer to God. *Jehovah* was dropped as the name for the Deity—or, as the revisers expressed it, "the committee agreed immediately and unanimously to 'return unto the Lord.'" [14] Archaic words and idioms were modernized. For example, where the King James Bible says that Joseph "was minded to put her [Mary] away privily," the Revised Standard Version says that he "resolved to divorce her quietly."

Virtually all Protestant scholars agree that this Bible is the most nearly accurate translation ever made. Although some readers have objected to its changing of the wording (and often the sense) of many a time-honored passage, the high degree of accuracy in the Revised Standard rendering commends itself to modern scholarship. Furthermore, this version clarifies many passages which no other English version has ever made clear. Though inferior to the King James Bible in beauty of expression and magnificence of language, the Revised Standard Version is invaluable as a much more accurate rendering of the Scriptures.

Although the traditional chapter-and-verse divisions are retained, prose passages are divided into paragraphs as determined by the sense of the passage. Quotation marks appear wherever modern usage dictates. Footnotes (citing parallel passages, giving variant readings, or calling attention to some emendation or to some uncertainty of translation) are placed at the bottom of the page. The summary of each chapter, found in the King James Version, is omitted, but a very brief indication of the contents of each page is found at the top of the page. A typographical distinction is made between poetry and prose.

The New English Bible (1961). In 1947 the Church of Scotland, the Church of England, and various Free Churches of England organized a committee to arrange for a new translation of the Bible in the light of all the known facts concerning the linguistic and historical development of Biblical literature. Three groups of translators (one group each for the Old Testament, the Apocrypha, and the New Testament) have been collaborating in the work; a fourth group has provided guidance concerning literary style and linguistic problems. The principal aim has been that of reproducing clearly the meaning and general effect of the Biblical passages by means of modern, accurate, and dignified expression. The translation of the New Testament, completed and approved in 1960, was published in 1961 jointly by the Cambridge University Press and the Oxford University Press. The modern tone of the text aroused heated controversy. Favorable comment emphasized the simplicity and clarity of the translation; unfavorable comment deplored the loss of power and the lack of authoritative tone. Both the supporters and the critics have eagerly awaited release of the translation of the Old Testament.

3

The Founding of the Hebrew Nation

The scope of Biblical history is very broad. The historical and biographical books of the Old Testament trace the history of the Hebrew people (with some gaps) from the creation of the world down through the rebuilding of Jerusalem after the return from the Babylonian Exile (*c.* 400 B.C.). Then after an interval of slightly more than two centuries, the story is resumed in the Apocryphal I and II Maccabees, which tell about the Hebrew rebellion (*c.* 167-134 B.C.) against Antiochus Epiphanes and his successors. Finally, the biographical and historical books of the New Testament relate the life of Jesus Christ and the history of the early church to about A.D. 65.

BIBLICAL SOURCES

The various authors of this comprehensive history drew on many different sources. For information about the earliest centuries (before *c.* 1000 B.C.), the historiographers had to rely almost entirely on oral tradition—myths,* legends, accounts of famous battles, scraps of folksongs, and the like—all handed down by

* A *myth* is a traditional story about a god or demigod or about the origin of the world or of people and things on it; to the non-orthodox scholar, the myth has no factual basis. A *legend* is a tale about some national, racial, or tribal hero or event; generally it contains some basis in fact, but the events related are ordinarily exaggerated or falsely ascribed to the persons involved; often it is difficult to distinguish between the historical and the fictional elements in a legend. Both myths and legends fall under the general heading of *folklore,* which includes, in addition, folksongs, oracles, and folk riddles. The usual characteristics of folklore are anonymity, spontaneity, objectivity, evidence of communal interest, imagination, irony, and humor. (Summarized from Laura H. Wild, *A Literary Guide to the Bible.* New York: Harper and Brothers, 1922, pp. 22-32.)

word of mouth, perhaps for many generations. The oldest *written* records on which the Biblical historians depended were probably codes of laws, such as the original Mosaic form of the Ten Commandments. Near the beginning of the tenth century B.C., it is believed, a priest began writing down an account of current happenings at the court of King David, many of which the priest himself had witnessed; this practice apparently continued intermittently for several centuries. Some later works consisted of personal memoirs, such as those of Nehemiah. Considered all together, the historical and biographical books of the Bible show a fairly continuous evolution in the direction of accuracy and authenticity—an evolution from those books which depended upon tradition and legend, through those which relied upon law codes and court records, to those which to a large extent were made up of diaries and transcriptions of eyewitness accounts.

THE BIBLE AS HISTORY

The student of the Bible should remember that the conception of history as a scientifically accurate record of events is a relatively modern idea. It simply never occurred to some of the ancient Jewish historians that it was incumbent upon them to investigate the reliability of their sources, to weed out all information that might be biased, and to distinguish between hearsay evidence and verifiable fact. Their primary concern was to present each religious truth as they saw it (often as miraculous truth governed by divine intervention) and to bring that truth home to the reader by any literary means that came to hand. They thought and wrote emotionally and figuratively. Hence some of their writings may contain more of *poetic* truth than statistical or historical evidence.

Most Biblical scholars today believe, for example, that Ruth and Esther are fictional narratives, each with a distinct purpose of its own. Some commentators have suggested that the accounts of Creation in Genesis are mythological and that Adam and Eve symbolize mankind and womankind but were never intended to be regarded as a particular man and a particular woman. A number of critics have held that the "tall tales" about Samson belong to the realm of legend rather than to the realm of history. Many scholars believe that some of the stories about such patriarchs as

Reuben and Judah should be interpreted as referring not to the patriarchs themselves but to the *tribes* of which they were the progenitors. And, finally, nearly all students of the Bible recognize that the dates, the vital statistics, and the chronology of events as given in the Old Testament and the Apocrypha are often inconsistent from the modern point of view—or at least are often based on methods of calculating time which were probably quite different from our own.

Despite the presence of much nonhistorical matter, there is, of course, a great deal of real history to be found in the Bible. In fact, written records of neighboring lands, such as Egypt, Assyria, Greece, and Rome, and archaeological discoveries made in Palestine itself corroborate many of the accounts given by Biblical historians.

A very ancient tradition, going back perhaps as far as the fifth century B.C.,[1] ascribed the composition of the first five Biblical books (the Pentateuch) to Moses; and a somewhat later tradition claimed the hero Joshua to be the author of the book which bears his name. Modern scholars believe that the Mosaic passages, having been transmitted as oral tradition, were repeatedly reinterpreted and supplemented until the composite work (the six books of the Hexateuch) was complete in its final form.

THE FIVE DOCUMENTS

Repetitions, inconsistencies, chronological difficulties, and differences in style within the long narrative indicate that the compilers of the Hexateuch were relying on more than one source.[2] Intensive scholarly investigation has led to the identification of five principal documents: J, E, D, H, P.

The J Document.* At some time between 950 and 850 B.C.[3] a scribe (or scribes) steeped in the tradition of the southern tribes (Judah and Benjamin) wrote a history of the Hebrews covering the period from Creation down to the last years of the reign of King David. This document emphasized (1) the peculiar relationship between God and the Israelites, his "Chosen People";

---

* So called because the document uses the Hebrew letters YHVH (the "Tetragrammaton") as the name of the Deity; German scholars used the letter J to represent the Hebrew letter *yodh*, the first of the four Hebrew letters. Some English renderings of the Tetragrammaton are *Yahweh, Yahveh,* and *Jehovah* (American Standard Version).

(2) the legends and traditions of the southern tribes; and (3) the importance of Hebron, David's first capital.[4] "J" (as both the document and its author are called) has a primitive and anthropomorphic conception of God, and he stresses the importance of sacrificial offerings. He is an excellent storyteller; his narratives move dramatically and swiftly, and they abound in graphic and concrete details. His material may be found in Genesis, Exodus, Leviticus, Numbers, Joshua, Judges, and (probably) I and II Samuel. Some specimens of his writing are The Story of Creation (as given in Gen. 2:4-26); The Tower of Babel Story (Gen. 11:1-9); and the Story of Abraham, Sarah, and Lot (Gen. 18:1–19:28).[5]

The E Document.* About 700 B.C.,[6] soon after the Assyrians had overwhelmed the Northern Kingdom (Israel), an author now designated "E" reworked the J Document and included a new set of traditions—those followed by a group from the north, whose center of worship was probably Shechem. E shows less anthropomorphism and more didacticism than J, and his history is more systematic, logical, refined, and elaborate than that of J. Material from the E Document may be found in Genesis, Exodus, Numbers, and Joshua, and perhaps in Judges, I and II Samuel, and I and II Kings. Some examples of E narrative are The Sacrifice of Isaac (Gen. 22:1-19), Moses in the Bulrushes (Ex. 2:1-10), and Moses and Jethro (Ex. 18).[7]

The D Document.† In 621 B.C., during the reign of Josiah, king of Judah, a book of law was found in the Temple at Jerusalem (II Kings 22:8). It is now believed that this book was partially or perhaps wholly identical with our book of Deuteronomy.[8] Its date has been placed at some time between 722 and 621 B.C. Its contents consist of rules for religious practices, and its emphasis is on the purification of worship by recognizing the Temple at Jerusalem as the only sanctuary of God. "D" (also known as "the Deuteronomist") has a lofty style. It is believed that he wrote not only all (or most) of Deuteronomy but also about half of Joshua.

The H Document.†† About 570 B.C. an unidentified scribe or priest compiled some rules for ethical and ceremonial guidance.

---

* So called because the author uses the word *Elohim* for the Deity.
† So called because it furnished the "Deuteronomic Code."
†† So called because it provides us with the "Holiness Code."

This document of rules, now known as the "Holiness Code," is approximately identical with Leviticus 17–26.

The P Document.* About 500 B.C., after the return from the Babylonian Exile, the priests at Jerusalem felt the need to consolidate and systematize Jewish religious law and history, to provide a unified constitution or manifesto for the restored Hebrew nation. They felt obligated to preserve the sacred material of the J, E, D, and H documents, but they rewrote some of it and added new portions of their own. They avoided anthropomorphisms and softened some passages they regarded as too harsh or otherwise objectionable. Their emphasis was on ritual and on instruction in the letter of the Law. They aimed at preciseness and accuracy, and they zealously recorded dates, measurements, catalogues, and genealogies. The style of the P Document is dry, formal, prosaic, and methodical, full of mannerisms and stereotyped phrases. There are, however, some lofty and magnificent passages—for example, the Story of Creation as found in the first chapter of Genesis. Material from this document appears in Genesis, Exodus, Leviticus, Numbers, and Joshua.[9]

About 350 B.C., or perhaps slightly earlier, the entire material of five documents was re-edited and put into approximately the form in which we have it today. Such was the development of the Hexateuch, "a work of such range and power as to seem to most people the supreme and characteristic creation of the Hebrew genius." [10]

GENESIS †

"In the beginning God created the heaven and the earth." Writers of classical Greek literature might have expressed this initial idea of Genesis as follows: "In the beginning there was only chaos, whence came Mother Earth, Love, and Night." Or one of the authors of a collection of great Germanic literature might have expressed the same idea this way: "Once there was only a bottomless pit, a world of mist, and a world of light." What a difference between those two sentences and the opening sentence of the Bible! The first four words of Genesis strike the keynote of the whole Bible: "In the beginning God. . . ." There-

---

* So called because it is the work of priests.
† The word *Genesis* is of Greek derivation and means "beginning."

after the priestly authors dramatically unroll the process of Creation: of light, of heaven, of the earth with its grass and herbs and trees, of the seas, of the sun and the moon and stars, of birds and fish and animals, and finally of man, the most wonderful of God's creatures. Light was created prior to the formation of the sun, moon, and stars. God created all in six days but rested on the seventh, instituting the Sabbath. Simplicity and brevity intensify the drama and impact of the story. The reader feels that elaboration or explanation (attempted in some translations) inevitably weakens the force of the original.

Thus the book of Genesis starts with the origin of the universe; it continues the story to a point roughly estimated to be about 1600 B.C.[11] The book falls logically into two parts: (1) accounts pertaining to the era from Creation to the advent of Abraham (1:1–11:9); and (2) stories of the patriarchs Abraham, Isaac, Jacob, and Joseph (11:10–50:26).

The Mythological Cycle (1:1–11:9). A Biblical myth is an account of material phenomena to explain their divine origins and development. In this sense, to the non-orthodox scholar the first eleven chapters of Genesis are chiefly mythological. This portion of the book answers the questions that primitive man everywhere has always asked: Where did the earth and the planets come from? How did man get here, what is his nature, and why does he have so many troubles? How did different races and different languages originate? In answering these questions, these eleven chapters are concerned with mankind in general rather than with only the Hebrews. Not till the introduction of Abraham at the end of Chapter 11 does Genesis become specifically an account of the Jewish people.

THE TWO ACCOUNTS OF CREATION (1:1–2:3 and 2:4-26). Two distinct accounts of Creation are given in Genesis. The first (1:1–2:3), from the P Document, is a very orderly story: on each of the first six days God creates a different class of things; then on the seventh he rests. As for the human race, we are told very simply that "God created man in his own image, in the image of God created he him; male and female created he them." The author marvels at God's power and rejoices over the whole process: "And God saw that it was good." The second story (2:4-26), from the J Document, is less elaborate (considered by some more anthropomorphic) than the preceding one: there is no division of the work into days, and of the creation of man we are told merely that the "Lord God formed man of the dust of the ground, and breathed into his nostrils the breath of life; and man became a living soul." It is to this second document, however, that we owe the story of the Garden of Eden (2:8-15), the name "Adam," and the account of the creation of Eve from Adam's rib. Monogamy is represented as God's law of marriage.

THE FALL OF MAN (3:1-24). Adam has been forbidden to eat the fruit of only one tree in Eden, the Tree of Knowledge; if he eats its fruit, he shall "surely die." The serpent tempts Eve with the fruit, assuring her that she not only will continue to live but also will grow wiser, so that she will be "as gods, knowing good and evil." Eve eats some of the fruit and gives some to Adam. God declares the penalties to be imposed for this disobedience: for Eve, the pain of child-bearing and subservience to her husband; for Adam, a life of hard labor ending in death. Then God drives Adam and Eve from Eden back to the western land of their origin where they must till the soil in hardship to obtain sustenance. (The text [3:22] states another reason for the expulsion, namely, God's fear that Adam might eat the fruit of the Tree of Life and become divinely immortal.)

THE FIRST MURDER (4:1-15). The story of the first murder possibly is meant to illustrate a conflict between the two ancient occupations of farming and sheepherding. Cain and Abel, the sons of Adam and Eve, are respectively a farmer and a keeper of sheep. The sacrificial offering of the sinful Cain is rejected by God, whereas that of the good Abel is accepted. In jealous anger Cain waylays Abel in the field and slays him. Here the author gives a fine psychological portrait of the guilty Cain: "And the Lord said unto Cain, 'Where is Abel thy brother?' And he said, 'I know not: Am I my brother's keeper?'" Then the Lord states the penalty for the murder: the earth no longer responds to Cain's efforts to cultivate it, and he will live in exile as a permanent "vagabond in the earth." Sin follows the family history: thus, one of Cain's descendants practices polygamy contrary to lawful precedents (4:19).

STORIES ABOUT NOAH (6:1—9:29). After some genealogies* of the generations from Adam to Noah come two stories about the

* One of the most famous of the people mentioned in the genealogies is Methuselah (5:21-22, 25-27), who is said to have lived 969 years. Popular

latter. The first, the famous story of the Flood, closely resembles a Babylonian story, and there are more or less parallel accounts in the mythologies of many races. Briefly summarized, the narrative in Genesis is as follows: When God perceives that mankind has become wicked, he decides to destroy all men except the righteous Noah and his family. Obeying God's instructions, Noah builds an ark and takes into it his family (including the wives of his three sons) and a male and a female of each species of created animals. Every other living thing is destroyed by rains which last "forty * days and forty nights." At length a dove proves that the flood is subsiding by finding and bringing back to the ark a live olive twig. God sends a rainbow † as a sign of his promise never to punish mankind with such a flood again. Noah's three sons became the fathers of all mankind.

The second tale about Noah (9:20-27) was probably told to justify the Hebrews' enslavement of the Canaanites: Ham, one of Noah's sons and progenitor of the Canaanites, discovers his father drunk and "uncovered within his tent." He tells his two brothers, Shem and Japheth, about the spectacle; but they modestly refuse to view their father's nakedness, and, walking backward with averted gaze, they cover him up. On awakening, Noah curses Ham and condemns him and his descendants to be servants to the other two sons and their descendants. The existence of this tale explains why the medieval mystery plays and Marc Connelly's *Green Pastures* depict Noah as a bit too fond of the bottle.

In the medieval play *The Deluge* the story is embellished with gaiety as Mrs. Noah is pictured as refusing to board the

---

tradition holds that he lived longer than anybody else ever has. The chronology given in Chapters 5–7 shows that Methuselah died in the year of Noah's Flood. Hence some scholars have concluded from this portion of Genesis that Methuselah was drowned in the Flood.

* "Forty" is a round number often used in the Bible to denote a considerable quantity. The Israelites wander forty years in the wilderness (Nu. 14:33 and 32:13), Eli judges Israel forty years (I Sam. 4:18), David and Solomon reign forty years each (I Kings 2:11 and 11:42), and so on.

† It has been suggested that the rainbow symbolized God's bow from which he shot the arrows of lightning. Hence the appearance of the rainbow in the sky represents a laying aside of God's weapon of wrath against mankind. See Cuthbert A. Simpson, exegesis to Genesis, *The Interpreter's Bible* (New York: Abingdon-Cokesbury Press, 1952), I, 551.

ark and has to be pushed into it. Noah complains about the stubborness of all women. Another medieval play, the Wakefield *Noah,* depicts a similar situation in which Noah and his wife quarrel and exchange hefty blows. In general, both medieval and modern plays on Biblical themes are mere stories in contrast to the vivid tales in the Old Testament which are related as historical events controlled by God for his inexorable purpose. Therefore the Biblical language is brief, simple, direct, and sober, with little or no embellishment.

THE TOWER OF BABEL (11:1-9). In the course of time, men again become proud and excessively ambitious. Their pride leads them to build the Tower of Babel, which is to be so high that its top will reach heaven. Foreseeing the lengths to which their vanity and ambition might drive them, God causes the men (who are "of one language and of one speech") to speak different languages and scatters them over the face of the earth.

Legends of Four Hebrew Patriarchs. The second division of Genesis consists of biographical stories of the four earliest Hebrew patriarchs.

ABRAHAM (12:1–25:8).* Abraham (originally called Abram †), a descendant of Shem, is so devout and God-fearing, so righteous and trustworthy, that God selects him to be the progenitor of his "Chosen People." Abraham's birthplace was Ur of the Chaldees, whence his family had taken him to live in Haran. Now directing him to leave Haran and go to Canaan, the Lord promises to make of Abraham's descendants "a great nation" and a blessing to all other nations. This promise (12:2-3) is the beginning of the "Covenant" between God and the Hebrews which is to play a very significant role in the religious life of the people. The Covenant is repeated in 15:1-21 and again in 17:1-8. Although there is nowhere in Genesis a description of Abraham's obligations under the Covenant, there is an implication (17:9 ff.) that God will keep his promise to the Chosen People only so long as they worship him, keep his commandments, and live

* Because the stories of Abraham, Isaac, Jacob, and Joseph naturally overlap, so must the chapter-and-verse divisions given here. The birth of Abraham is announced in Gen. 11:26.

† Names had great significance. To know the name of something implied authority and power over it. God changed Abram's name to Abraham and with it changed his destiny.

righteous lives. (See reference to the Chosen People in Deut. 7:6: ". . . God hath chosen thee . . . above all people that are upon the face of the earth.")

Obeying God's order, Abraham moves to Canaan, taking with him his wife Sarah (originally named Sarai) and his nephew Lot and the latter's wife. Unable to obtain enough food in Canaan, the migrants go to Egypt where Abraham passes off Sarah as his sister (she was his half-sister)* to avoid being killed by the Egyptians on her account. (They would have murdered the husband of a woman they coveted.) Pharaoh takes Sarah into his house and gives Abraham gifts but later discovers the truth and expels the migrants from Egypt.

Returning to Canaan, the two families find that there is insufficient grazing land in a single area to support them. Abraham, knowing that the families must separate, magnanimously gives Lot first choice of the region in which to settle. Lot chooses the plain of Jordan, and settles down in Sodom, while Abraham establishes his household on the plain of Mamre in the Hebron area—a place later to become famous as David's first capital.

After dwelling in Canaan for ten years, Abraham still has had no offspring. (It was customary at this time for a barren wife to provide her husband with a slave as a concubine who never, however, attained the legal status of a wife. Eventually, bigamy came into frequent practice, and then the rights of offspring became matters of controversy.) Sarah persuades him to take as a second wife Hagar, her Egyptian maid, who becomes pregnant. A family quarrel ensues: Hagar is contemptuous of Sarah's barrenness, and Sarah retaliates by mistreating her. Hagar flees to the wilderness, where a son, Ishmael, is born. (This episode could be interpreted as an explanation for the enmity between the Israelites and the Ishmaelites, Bedouins living in the deserts south of Palestine.)

Next is a story which is the first of a series of Biblical narratives concerning childless women to whom the Lord grants the gift of bearing a child.† God tells Abraham that Sarah is going to bear him a son. Both Abraham and his wife laugh in disbelief

* This story of passing off his wife as his sister appears three times in Genesis (12:13; 20:2; 26:7).

† Compare the conceptions of Samson (Judges 13:2-7), of Samuel (I Sam. 1:4-23), and of John the Baptist (Luke 1:5-24).

at the prospect, for Sarah is ninety years old, while her husband says he is a hundred (17:17).* Despite their old age, however, Sarah conceives and gives birth to Isaac.

Meanwhile, Sodom and its neighbor city Gomorrah have become so wicked that God decides to destroy them. Abraham, trying to save Sodom, scolds God for injustice to the good people there, but the Lord rejects his protest because not even ten righteous men could be found in the city. Righteous Lot and his family are told to flee from Sodom. As her punishment for disobeying God's injunction that during their flight they must not watch the destruction of the cities (by "brimstone and fire"), Lot's wife is turned into a pillar of salt (19:26).

Another account tells that Lot's two daughters make their father drunk, cohabit with him, and bear him two sons, who are to become the ancestors of the Moabites and the Ammonites; thus the historian explains the origins of two of the traditional enemies of the Israelites.

In obedience to God's command, when Isaac is eight days old Abraham has him circumcised as a sign of the Covenant between God and Abraham's descendants. In this way Abraham institutes the important Jewish tradition of circumcision.[12]

Upon the death of Sarah (Chapter 23), Abraham buys a plot of ground near Hebron in which to bury her body.† He later remarries and has sons by his second wife and his concubines; his favorite son is Isaac, to whom he leaves all his possessions when he dies at the "good old age" of 175.

IsAAC (21:1–22:13, 24:1-67, and 35:28-29). Concerning the character of Isaac, the second of the Jewish patriarchs, the Bible has little to say. He seems to be a nondescript figure who is presented only in relation to his father and his sons.

A highly dramatic story, one of the most profoundly moving in all literature, is told concerning the young Isaac. To test Abraham's loyalty and faith, God commands him to slay the boy and to make of his body a sacrificial offering. "Take now thy son, thine only son Isaac, whom thou lovest, . . . and offer him . . .

---

* He was actually ninety-nine.

† Centuries later, after the return from the Babylonian Exile, this purchase was to furnish legalistic grounds for the Israelites' claim to this portion of Canaan, then occupied by the Edomites. (Simpson, exegesis, *The Interpreter's Bible*, I, 647.)

for a burnt offering. . . ." The devout old man prepares to slaughter his only son, on whom rests his sole hope for the future of the family; the boy helps in the preparation, ignorant of his father's intentions. When Isaac turns to ask: "Behold the fire and the wood: but where is the lamb for a burnt offering?" Abraham replies: "My son, God will provide himself a lamb for a burnt offering." Such faith and obedience are rewarded: as the father takes the knife to kill his son, an angel stops him. Then Abraham sees a ram caught in a thicket by his horns; he sacrifices the ram as a burnt offering instead of his son. God renews the promise to multiply Abraham's descendants and make them victorious "because thou hast obeyed my voice"—a fitting conclusion to a story filled with dramatic challenge, suspense, and deep emotion. (Note, however, that throughout the history of the Hebrew people human sacrifice was rejected as being contrary to their religion; even the sacrifice of animals was often condemned insofar as it became a substitute for obedience to God's laws.) It is useful to contrast the medieval Brome play *Abraham and Isaac* with this Biblical account. The play exaggerates the child's emotions ("I pray you, father, change your face, and kill me not with your knife") and ends with a moralizing epilogue. Despite the high literary quality of medieval and modern literature using a Biblical theme, how much more eloquent and dramatic is the simple, straightforward Old Testament story which carries its own convincing moral lesson!

Isaac grows to manhood, and his father seeks a suitable wife for him. The discovery and winning of Rebekah is a beautiful pastoral idyl (Chapter 24).

JACOB (ISRAEL) (25:19–35:29). The biography of the third of the patriarchs is a saga of greed, envy, and shrewd treachery.

Soon after Rebekah becomes pregnant, she feels two children struggling in her womb (apparently against each other). Considering this an omen, she asks God what it means, and he tells her that she is to give birth to twins who will be the forefathers of two rival nations. (This incident serves as an explanation of the origin of the traditional enmity between the Hebrews, the descendants of Jacob, and the Edomites, the descendants of Esau.) At the moment the twins are born, the animosity continues, for Jacob is holding on to the foot of Esau, the firstborn. When they reach manhood, twice Jacob practices his wiles on his elder brother. First, he catches Esau in a weak moment, when Esau comes in from the field faint with hunger. Jacob refuses him food except in exchange for his birthright—that is, for Esau's rightful place as heir to the headship of the family. Esau concedes and thus sells his birthright for a "mess of pottage." Then, second, abetted by his mother, Jacob conspires to cheat Esau of his father's blessing. Now, Isaac is partial to Esau, the hairy, masculine huntsman, who brings him savory venison; Rebekah, on the other hand, prefers Jacob, the smooth-skinned "plain man, dwelling in tents." When Isaac (now blind with age) sends Esau out to hunt game and tells him to prepare it in his customary way, Rebekah disguises Jacob by dressing him in Esau's clothes and by putting hairy goatskins on his hands and neck so that he will feel like Esau; she also prepares savory meat to be served to Isaac. Jacob lies about his identity as he approaches his father; Isaac feels the hairy hands, smells the clothes, eats the meat, and is convinced that Jacob is Esau. He blesses Jacob and makes him lord over his brothers. The moment of Esau's return is a dramatic one. When he perceives that he has been cheated, he cries "with a great and exceeding bitter cry" (27:34). Isaac blesses him, too, but cannot revoke the decrees making Jacob head of the clan.

In order to escape Esau's murderous wrath, Jacob flees to Haran and becomes the servant of his uncle Laban, Rebekah's brother. En route he sees in a dream a vision of a ladder reaching to heaven, on which angels are ascending and descending. God appears at the top of the ladder and renews the promises he has made to Abraham and Isaac; Jacob vows faithfulness to God (27:41–28:22).

Jacob falls in love with Laban's pretty young daughter Rachel. Her father agrees to the match provided Jacob will labor for him for seven years. At the end of the time Laban proves as untrustworthy and as guileful as his sister Rebekah. He requires Jacob to marry Leah, the unattractive, "weak-eyed" older sister of Rachel and to labor seven more years before he can marry his beloved. At the end of the fourteen years Laban again proves dishonest by trying to cheat Jacob of his sheep, but this time Jacob outwits the uncle and departs for his native region with Leah, Rachel, and much wealth (29:1–31:55).

By this point Jacob has shown pretty well what his characteristics and abilities are. His most obvious trait is craftiness, derived, no doubt, from his mother.* In addition to craftiness, Jacob is endowed with tremendous strength and hardihood: he uses a rock as a pillow (Gen. 28:11), he single-handedly rolls a great rock from a well (29:10), and he wrestles successfully with a supernatural being (32:24-30) later referred to as God himself ("I have seen God face to face, and my life is preserved"). God changes Jacob's name to Israel (32:28-30), which means "contender with God." Jacob is also patient (witness the fourteen years of labor for Rachel), and he is capable of great parental love (see below the accounts of his affection for Joseph and Benjamin). His best characteristic is his unswerving faith in God (see, for example, 28:16, 31:5-16, and 32:9-12).

Fearing now that Esau may still seek revenge for his former injuries, Jacob sends him a series of presents. Esau forgives him, the two are reconciled, and Jacob settles down to rear a large family and to accumulate great riches (32:1–33:15).

Jacob begets twelve sons and one daughter: (1) Leah bears Reuben, Simeon, Levi, Judah, Issachar, Zebulun, and the daughter, Dinah; (2) Rachel bears Joseph and Benjamin; (3) Bilhah, Rachel's maidservant, bears Dan and Naphtali; and (4) Zilpah, Leah's maidservant, bears Gad and Asher. The sons are of prime importance in Jewish history. Ten of them (Levi and Joseph excepted) lend their names to ten of the well-known "tribes of Israel." (Levi's descendants, though called a tribe, are set aside as a priestly group, and Joseph's two sons, Ephraim and Manasseh, become the progenitors of two "half-tribes.") The suffix -ite is attached to the name of the head of each tribe to indicate a descendant; for example, a Danite is a descendant of Dan, a Benjamite is a descendant of Benjamin, and so on.

JOSEPH (37:1–50:26). Many commentators have remarked that the story of Joseph is one of the most skillfully told narratives in the Bible. To an anthropologist and a student of folklore, the exciting plot resembles that of the universally popular tale of Cinderella, with Joseph as the mistreated protagonist, the elder

---

* This trait seems to be admired by the author of this portion of Genesis and by some other Biblical authors; see, for example the tales about Ehud, Jael, and Gideon in Judges 3 and 5–7. Many later writers of Biblical books, however, deplore anything that smacks of trickery and deceit; see especially Jer. 5:2, Amos 8:5, Mark 7:22, and Romans 1:29.

brothers corresponding to the cruel stepmother and stepsisters, and Pharaoh playing the part of the fairy godmother. Of course, to the orthodox scholar, the theme of the Joseph story seems to be much more serious and elevated than that of Cinderella, for the Biblical tale illustrates how God sometimes works in obscure and mysterious ways to preserve his Chosen People; it also accounts for the Israelites' presence in Egypt about 1600 B.C.

In many respects Joseph is the most attractive of the four patriarchs. Since he was the first son of Jacob's beloved wife Rachel (ten others being sons of Leah, whom Jacob did not love, or of the servants), Jacob loved him best of all his twelve sons. As an adult Joseph is so chaste that he refuses to be seduced by another man's wife; he is so astute an administrator that Pharaoh places him in charge of all the food supplies in Egypt; and he is of so tender and forgiving a nature that he holds no grudge against his brothers for selling him into slavery.

The ten oldest sons of Jacob, resentful of the partiality which their father shows to Joseph and also of Joseph's dreams exalting him above his brothers, decide to kill the boy: "Behold, this dreamer cometh. Come now . . . let us slay him. . . ." But Reuben persuades the others to throw Joseph into a pit instead, intending to rescue him later; then Judah suggests selling the boy to a caravan of merchants en route to Egypt. This they do (without Reuben's knowledge), then dip Joseph's coat, or long-sleeved robe (given to him by his father), in the blood of an animal and bring it home to Jacob, telling him that Joseph has been killed by a wild animal.

The merchants sell Joseph to Potiphar, captain of Pharaoh's guard. Potiphar's wife tries to seduce Joseph. When he remains loyal to the captain and rejects her advances, she tells Potiphar that Joseph has tried to seduce her. To substantiate her accusation, she shows him a garment which Joseph has left in her grasp when he fled from the house. "The Hebrew servant . . . came in unto me to mock me: And it came to pass, as I lifted up my voice and cried, that he left his garment with me, and fled out" (39:17-18). Joseph is thrown into prison, but even there he prospers: he wins the favor of the keeper, who puts him in charge of all the other prisoners. Pharaoh's head butler and baker are also in prison and have strange dreams which Joseph correctly interprets. Eventually Pharaoh frees the butler but hangs the baker, as predicted by Joseph. Later the monarch himself has two dreams which his magicians are unable to interpret: one, that seven fat cows were devoured by seven lean ones, and another, that seven plump ears of grain were eaten by seven blighted ones. Joseph interprets the dreams of Pharaoh to mean that there will be seven years of prosperity followed by seven years of famine. He advises Pharaoh to store up great supplies of food during the "fat" years. Impressed by Joseph's abilities, Pharaoh makes him overseer of all Egypt (41:40-44).

The dreams come true, and only Egypt has food during the "lean" years. Driven by famine in Canaan, Joseph's ten older brothers come to Egypt to buy grain. Joseph knows who they are and is filled with love for them. They, however, do not recognize this exalted official as their brother. He sells them grain, but tells them not to come back for more without bringing with them their youngest brother, Benjamin, who has replaced Joseph as Jacob's favorite son. When a second trip to Egypt is necessary, the brothers bring Benjamin with them, much against their father's wishes. Again Joseph sells them grain, but this time he has his own silver cup put into Benjamin's bag. Then he sends his servants to accuse the brothers of stealing the cup. When it is discovered in Benjamin's bag, Judah implores Joseph to let him become Joseph's servant (as a penalty) in Benjamin's stead. Overcome by emotion, Joseph breaks into tears, reveals his identity, and is reconciled with his brothers. Jacob is brought from Canaan to spend the remainder of his days with all his sons in Egypt.

Especially memorable are the passages relating the following events: (1) Reuben's discovery that Joseph is not in the pit (37:29-30); (2) Jacob's sorrow over Joseph's reported death (37:34-35); (3) the brothers' humbling themselves before Joseph in Egypt and his various schemes to confuse and try them (42:6-34); (4) the attempts by Judah to protect Benjamin (44:22 and 44:32-34); and (5) the scene of revelation and reconciliation (45:1-15).

Jacob (now known as Israel) and his family settle in the fertile Egyptian land of Goshen. The Egyptians are compelled by famine to sell their lands to Joseph, as Pharaoh's agent. He makes slaves of them, introducing universal slavery, and establishes a 20 per cent levy on production. But Jacob's family prosper. In a famous passage Jacob blesses his twelve sons and the two sons of Joseph, namely, Ephraim and Manasseh * (48:10—49:27). The book closes with the deaths respectively of Jacob and of Joseph. At a future date (as recorded in Exodus 13:19) the Israelites show their reverence for the memory of Joseph by carrying his remains with them on their journey from Egypt to Canaan.

EXODUS

The word *Exodus*, a Greek derivative, means "the going out." As applied to the second book of the Hexateuch, it refers to the epic passage of the children of Israel from Egypt to Canaan— a passage regarded by many scholars as a historical fact. This book covers the period from the death of Joseph in Egypt to the building and dedication of the Tabernacle in the wilderness. It has three main divisions: the period of bondage in Egypt (1:1—15:21), the journey to Mount Sinai (15:22—19:25), and events at Mount Sinai (20:1—40:38). The first two divisions are chiefly narrative, and, dominated as they are by the towering figure of Moses, they are literarily almost equal to the book of Genesis. The last section contains some excellent narrative and descriptive passages, but it is made up largely of laws and rules, which (though of great religious, ethical, and cultural significance) are of secondary importance as literature.

Bondage in Egypt and Escape from Bondage (1:1—15:21). "Now there arose up a new king over Egypt, which knew not Joseph." This sentence (which has become proverbial) marks a drastic change in the fortunes of the Israelites. After more than four hundred years (Ex. 12:40), the descendants of Jacob have become a multitude: "and the land was filled with them." The new Pharaoh [13] so fears their power that he orders not only the extremely harsh enslavement of the Hebrews but also the drowning of each newborn Hebrew male.

THE BIRTH OF MOSES (2:1-10). One of the women of the tribe of Levi saves her baby by putting him into a basket made of bulrushes, setting it afloat among the reeds at the edge of the river, and instructing her daughter Miriam to watch the basket from a distance.[14] The child is discovered by Pharaoh's daughter,

* Their mother was an Egyptian woman (Asenath) whom Pharaoh gave Joseph as his wife.

who takes pity on him and rescues him, even though she recognizes that he is a Hebrew. Miriam now comes forward and offers to find a nurse for the baby. When the princess accepts the offer, Miriam cleverly brings the baby's mother, whom Pharaoh's daughter pays to nurse him. Later Pharaoh's daughter adopts the boy and names him Moses, "because," she says, "I drew him out of the water." [15] Nothing else is told of the childhood of Moses.

MOSES' EXILE AND HIS CALLING BY GOD (2:11–4:28). The adult Moses is one of the most commanding and inspirational figures in the Old Testament. Writing about him six or eight centuries after his death, the Deuteronomist says: "And there arose not a prophet since in Israel like unto Moses, whom the Lord knew face to face" (Deut. 34:10). From the point of view of the orthodox scholar, this intimacy with God accounts in large measure for Moses' great power. "He was, in Spinoza's words, a *God-intoxicated* man and through that intoxication confirmed, one might better say *created*, in the Hebrew race that religious faith which was to endure after their life as a nation had died and to which we owe the religion of Christianity." [16] Moses is a superb combination of humility and boldness. He is humble, as is shown in his doubting his own ability (he is "slow of speech") to lead the Israelites out of bondage (Ex. 4:10); yet he is bold enough to upbraid God himself for giving him the burden of leading them. Two other traits of his are often seen together: quickness of temper and a "passionate sense of justice." Both of these are observable in his slaying of the Egyptian who is beating a Hebrew (Ex. 2:11-12) and his driving away of the shepherds who are mistreating Jethro's daughters (Ex. 2:16-17). Another characteristic that deserves mention is his patient perseverance, as seen in his dogged leading of the children of Israel through wilderness for forty years, despite their complaining and backsliding.

The first incident told about Moses as a man is the killing of an Egyptian. Moses flees to the land of Midian to escape punishment. There he marries Zipporah, the daughter of Jethro, a Midianite priest.* Moses remains in Midian "forty"years (according

* The Midianites (later to become enemies of the Hebrews) were a semi-nomadic people who lived southeast of Canaan.

to later chronology). Then the old king of Egypt dies; but his successor is equally oppressive to the Israelites, and the latter renew their cries to God for deliverance. God answers their prayers by choosing Moses as their deliverer. In a most impressive miraculous scene (3:2-6), Moses sees a fire in a bush in the wilderness, but the fire does not destroy the bush—"and, behold, the bush burned with fire, and the bush was not consumed." God tells Moses that he has chosen him to lead the Israelites out of Egypt into Canaan, "a land flowing with milk and honey." God promises to "smite Egypt with all my wonders" to force the Egyptians to let the Hebrews go. Moses objects that the people will not believe him; God answers his reluctance by enabling him to do miracles: Moses' rod turns into a serpent and his hand is smitten with leprosy; then both are restored. Again Moses objects that he is no speaker and therefore cannot sway the people with oratory; God promises that Aaron,* Moses' brother, who is a good orator, will be his spokesman. Moses obeys and returns to Egypt.

THE PLAGUES AND THE ESCAPE (4:29–15:21). Here is a dramatic story filled with suspense, conflict, and progressive action, including miracles, leading to the climax of victory. Moses and Aaron go up to Pharaoh and petition him to let the Hebrews go to the wilderness, but he haughtily refuses and says that the two petitioners are interfering with the Hebrews' labor. Moses threatens him with a plague—turning the water of the Egyptians to blood, and the plague is actually inflicted. Pharaoh's magicians duplicate the feat, and therefore the king remains obstinate. Then Moses calls down, one after another, eight more plagues: of frogs, gnats, flies, cattle-sickness, boils, hail, locusts, and darkness. Each time Egypt suffers from a plague, Pharaoh promises to let the children of Israel go, but becomes obdurate after the plague is removed. Now the Lord has reached the end of his patience with the Egyptians. He tells Moses to instruct each He-

---

* The Biblical historian's probable motive for mentioning the appointment of Aaron the Levite is to emphasize the divine ordination of the priesthood of Israel. "The passage seems to reflect strained relations between priest and prophet here represented by Moses in the writer's own day [700-450 B.C.?]." (J. Coert Rylaarsdam, exegesis to Exodus, *The Interpreter's Bible*, I, 879.

brew family to mark its doorposts and lintels with the blood of a lamb, because he is going to smite the first-born of every family in Egypt, "both man and beast," except those whose houses are so marked; these he will "pass over." The Lord gives a number of detailed instructions, such as the eating of unleavened bread for seven days. (Thus are explained the origins of both the Jewish festival of the Passover and the rite of Unleavened Bread.[17]) All happens as the Lord has promised, and great is the grief in the land of Egypt, "for there was not a house where there was not one dead." At last, Pharaoh allows the Israelites to depart and take their flocks and herds with them. Six hundred thousand men—in addition to the women and children—set out for Canaan.

God then hardens Pharaoh's heart so that Pharaoh regrets his decision to free the Hebrews and sends all his chariots and horsemen in pursuit. As the Hebrews, guided by a pillar of cloud by day and a pillar of fire by night (signs of the presence of God *), reach the Red Sea, God performs a glorious miracle to save them. He causes an east wind to blow all night and divide the waters so that there is a passageway of dry land through the sea. This enables the Hebrews to reach the shore, but in the morning when the Egyptians drive their chariots along the same passageway through the sea, God lets the waters come together again and drown them all.

Then Moses and the people sing their triumphant song (15:1-18), the opening words of which are perhaps the oldest piece of literature in the Bible.[18] It is an exultant lyric, and the opening is:

> I will sing unto the Lord, for he hath triumphed gloriously:
> The horse and his rider hath he thrown into the sea.

Contrast such terse, dramatic language with the medieval Caedmonian poem *Exodus* (c. A.D. 675), which pictures Moses as a Teutonic warrior as well as a lawgiver and relates how a heroic God intervened to assist the despondent Hebrews: "The waves mounted . . . blood-stained the flood . . . the fated men fell. . . ."

---

* Some scholars have sought to explain these phenomena by suggesting that Mount Sinai, toward which the Israelites were traveling, was a volcano and that the pillars of cloud and fire were the visible signs of an eruption. See J. Edgar Park, exposition to Exodus, *The Interpreter's Bible,* I, 931.

The medieval writers felt obliged to adapt, explain, and spell out the moral that the Egyptian armies were beaten because they "fought against God."

The Journey in the Wilderness to Sinai (15:22—19:25). After their escape the Israelites begin a "forty-year" period (commencing about 1200 B.C.) of wandering across deserts and wastelands. The initial phase, the journey to Mt. Sinai, is filled with hardships. Time after time they regret that they ever left the "fleshpots of Egypt," and they accuse Moses of leading them into the wilderness only to let them die there. Their first trial comes soon after they have crossed the Red Sea; they are thirsty, and they try the waters of Marah but find them bitter; Moses sweetens the waters by throwing a tree into them. Then the wanderers fear that they will starve to death, but God sends them initially a flock of quail and then a steady supply of manna, "the bread which the Lord hath given you to eat." Again they lack water, and Moses produces it by striking a rock in Horeb. Finally, they are attacked by the Amalekites.* The Hebrews find that they are victorious as long as Moses holds up his hands; Aaron and Hur, therefore, stand on each side of him and hold his hands up until the battle is won.

After a reunion with his wife, two sons, and father-in-law, Moses leads his people on to the foot of Mount Sinai (or Horeb).[19] There follows the highly dramatic story (accompanied by an eruptive volcano, thunder and lightning, and clouds from which issues the voice of God) that tells how the Lord summons Moses to the top of Mount Sinai and there proclaims the Ten Commandments and various ordinances (all written down by Moses) as well as two subsequent "tables of stone, written with the finger of God" (31:18).

Moses and the Giving of the Law (20:1—40:38). Therefore the last twenty-one chapters of Exodus contain not only the Ten Commandments but also the numerous other laws and rules. Some of the latter pertain to matters of universal interest, such as perjury, slander, charitableness, and legal justice. Others are of somewhat narrower interest, inasmuch as they deal with ceremonies, sacrifices, holy garments, the building of the Tabernacle,

---

* The Amalekites, who lived just north of Kadesh, were a tribe related to the Edomites. The reference here helps to account for the Israelites' age-old feud with them. See Rylaarsdam, *The Interpreter's Bible,* I, 959-960.

and the like. Though of great value to the student of history and religion, these laws are of lesser interest to the student of literature. It should be noted in passing, however, that despite approval of slavery and cruel punishment (e.g., "thou shalt not suffer a witch to live") these Hebrew laws are generally conceded to be more humanitarian than the laws of most other peoples of the same period. They require, for example, hospitality to strangers, kindness to widows and orphans, respect for the aged, and charity for the poor. One particular law has often been misinterpreted: "eye for eye, tooth for tooth," etc. (21:23-25), is a *limit* to which legally inflicted punishment can go—not an invitation of vengeance.[20] One other interesting law (28:30) requires the placing of the Urim and Thummin (oracles) in the breastplate of Aaron when he goes "before the Lord" in the Temple; these oracles were the Hebrew equivalent of pagan oracles and might be consulted upon practical issues.[21]

The Ten Commandments, of course, are the most significant laws given in the book; they and the narrative passages of this portion of Exodus require some comment here.

THE TEN COMMANDMENTS (20:1-17). The Ten Commandments form a code of laws for a pastoral and agricultural people; some analogous laws have been found in the codes of the ancient Egyptians and Babylonians. The age of the Ten Commandments is uncertain. Most scholars now believe that, though based on a shorter version attributed to Moses, some of them are of far later date and that in their later form they were inserted into the J or the E Document.[22] They outline two kinds of obligations: duties to God and duties to other men.[23] They may be briefly summarized as follows:

(1) Thou shalt have no gods except the Lord.

(2) Thou shalt not make or worship idols.

(3) Thou shalt not take the name of God in vain.*

---

* This commandment had special significance for the Hebrews, who used many devices in the Old Testament to avoid pronouncing the divine name. The use of God's name for ordinary matters implied lack of respect for his transcendence. In fact, they believed that somehow God's name expressed his character or power (see Rylaarsdam, exegesis, *The Interpreter's Bible,* I, 983). Belief in the efficacy of a proper name was held not only by the Hebrews but by people all over the world; proper names were widely used in invoking or exorcising various deities, spirits, devils, fairies, and the like.

  (4) Thou shalt keep the Sabbath day holy.
  (5) Thou shalt honor thy parents.*
  (6) Thou shalt not kill.
  (7) Thou shalt not commit adultery.
  (8) Thou shalt not steal.
  (9) Thou shalt not bear false witness (that is, commit perjury in court).
(10) Thou shalt not covet.

ESTABLISHMENT OF THE PRIESTHOOD: EPISODE OF THE MOLTEN CALF (28:1–32:35). Moses establishes a hereditary priesthood by appointing Aaron and his sons to be priests (28:1). Somewhat later (32:28-29) he consecrates the other Levites as priests (Aaron, too, it should be remembered, is a descendant of Levi; see 2:1).

While Moses is on Mount Sinai "forty days and forty nights" receiving from God the Ten Commandments and the so-called Code of the Covenant (Chapters 20–23), the Israelites break the Second Commandment. Wearied of waiting for their leader, they ask Aaron to make gods for them—palpable and visible gods. Aaron agrees and makes a golden calf † by melting down the earrings of the people. Informed by God of what has happened, Moses comes down from the mountain. So furious is he when he sees the people dancing about the golden calf that he breaks the stone tablets containing God's commandments—"written with the finger of God"! Furthermore, he burns the calf "in the fire," grinds it into powder, mixes the powder with water, and makes the people drink the mixture. He orders the slaying of 3,000 men:

The use may be seen in the old Germanic fairy tale about Rumpelstilzchen (who vanishes forever when he discovers that the queen has learned his strange name) and in Shakespeare's *Hamlet*, where the titular character employs various appellations to make his father's ghost communicate with him:

"I'll call thee Hamlet,
King, father, Royal Dane; O answer me . . ."

* Perhaps this commandment was included because of the nomadic custom of abandoning aged and dependent parents. See Rylaarsdam, exegesis, *The Interpreter's Bible*, I, 985.

† Calf-worship was a form of nature mysticism practiced in Canaan. Scholars believe that this story was not attached to the Moses cycle till after the eighth century B.C., when the people of the Kingdom of Israel were worshiping two golden calves, originally set up by Jeroboam I (see I Kings 12:28 and Rylaarsdam, exegesis, *The Interpreter's Bible*, I, 1063-1064).

"slay every man his brother and every man his companion, and every man his neighbor." God sends a plague upon the people as additional punishment for making the golden calf (32:35).

Conclusion (34:1–40:38). After Moses has prayed two intercessory prayers in behalf of the people (32:11-13 and 32:30-35), God relents and agrees to send an angel who will lead them to the Promised Land of Canaan. He reminds Moses of the Covenant made with Abraham: that God will prosper the Hebrews and make them a mighty and "chosen" people if they will worship him and obey his commandments. God "writes" the Ten Commandments again for Moses (34:1). When the great lawgiver returns to his people, the skin of his face shines because he has been talking with God (34:29).* Now an ark is built to house the Ten Commandments (virtually identified with the Covenant 24), and the ark is placed inside an elaborately constructed but portable tabernacle.25 The Ark of the Covenant is hereafter the holiest and most zealously guarded of the Israelites' religious paraphernalia.

The book ends with an awe-inspiring account of God's presence: "And Moses was not able to enter into the tent of the congregation, because the cloud abode thereon, and the glory of the Lord filled the tabernacle" (40:35). The children of Israel continue their journey only when the cloud is raised from the tabernacle. "For the cloud of the Lord was upon the tabernacle by day, and fire was on it by night, in the sight of all the house of Israel, throughout all their journeys" (40:38).

LEVITICUS

The word *Leviticus,* borrowed from the Septuagint, denotes "a book for the Levites." One should remember that Moses and Aaron were of the tribe of Levi (Ex. 2:1-2), that Moses consecrated all the Levites "to the service of the Lord" (Ex. 32:28-29), and that Moses ordained Aaron and his descendants to be priests (Ex. 28:1). In the early centuries, before the Babylonian Exile, the Levites (as distinguished from the Aaronites) perhaps performed some priestly functions: but between 586 B.C. and the

---

* Compare Christ's Transfiguration (Matt. 17:1-8). For the word *shone* (Ex. 34:29) the Vulgate used the translation "horned," whence the origin of the tradition that Moses had horns, as he is often represented in Renaissance paintings and in Michelangelo's famous piece of sculpture. See Park, exposition, *The Interpreter's Bible,* I, 1081.

end of Temple worship in A.D. 70 they "were the lower personnel of the sanctuary—assistants, gate-keepers, musicians, and the like —while the priests, through the ordination of Aaron and his sons, held final authority in matters of ritual."[26] Leviticus, however, was apparently a handbook not merely—or even principally— for the subordinate Levites, but for *all* the personnel who served within the Temple. Compiled more than seven centuries after the death of Moses, its purpose "seems to have been to project back into early times the highly developed ritual of the temple and to connect it with an early shrine, the tabernacle or trysting tent."[27] "It may be compared to those convenient casebooks which are composed for the benefit of students of the law. The volume itself will have a date, but its contents will be drawn from the legislation and judicial decisions of many generations."[28]

Most lawbooks make dull reading for the average person, and Leviticus is no exception. Its contents, however, are of considerable value to the student of religion, ethics, sociology, and Jewish history.[29]

The book may be divided into four sections: (1) Chapters 1—10, laws concerning sacrifices of animals (e.g., bulls, goats, sheep, or birds) and the consecration of the priesthood; (2) Chapters 11—16, laws concerning "cleanness," * purification (man being sinful and only God being holy), and atonement (Yom Kippur being the day reserved for fasting, special sacrifices, and penance); (3) Chapters 17—26, the Holiness Code,† which is the oldest section of Leviticus and is not so much concerned with priestly activities in the Temple as with holy feasts, social behavior, sexual behavior, and the observance of sabbatical and jubilee years (25:1-55); and (4) Chapter 27, laws concerning vows and tithes.

NUMBERS

The title of the fourth book of the Bible refers to the two "numberings" or censuses of the Israelites which are related in

* "Clean" and "unclean" are terms which have a special meaning in Jewish law. Many of the laws concerning cleanliness originated in the practice of hygiene, but "unclean" came to be applied to any "departure from prescribed practice" (Roy B. Chamberlin and Herman Feldman [eds.], *The Dartmouth Bible* [Boston: Houghton Mifflin Co., 2nd ed., 1961], p. 119).

† See below, p. 73 for a chart of the four codes found in the Pentateuch.

the book. The Hebrew title for the book, "In the Wilderness," is more accurate than the one found in the King James Bible. Only five chapters (1–4 and 26) are devoted to the taking of the census. Most of the other chapters tell about the thirty-nine years of wandering in the wilderness. Numbers begins where Exodus leaves off (at the departure of the Hebrews from Mount Sinai) and continues the narrative of migration till Israel has reached the outskirts of Moab. The first thirty-eight years of the journey are rather sketchily covered in the first nineteen chapters, whereas the account of the events of the final year of wandering fills seventeen chapters.

Though of greater literary interest than Leviticus, the book of Numbers contains much material which the average reader will willingly skip. For instance, Chapters 5, 6, 15, 18, and 19 record more rules and laws—laws concerning leprosy, adultery, jealousy, and trespassing, and rules pertaining to priestly and Levitical duties.

Only one of these chapters requires comment here. All of Chapter 6 is concerned with the preparation and consecration of a *Nazarite*. The word itself denotes one who is set apart or especially dedicated; here it is applied to one who has undertaken to keep three vows for a specified period. These vows are (1) to abstain from all alcoholic beverages—even from grapes, grape seeds, and skins, (2) to leave the head unshaven, and (3) to avoid touching or coming near a corpse. As we shall see later (in the discussion of the book of Judges), Samson the Nazarite kept the second of these vows but not the other two. Though not mentioned again in the Pentateuch, the Nazarites were numerous in later periods of Jewish history and are mentioned in Amos 2:11-12 and in I Maccabees 3:49.[30]

At the end of this section on the consecration of a Nazarite, the Lord dictates to Moses "the most beautiful benediction in the Scriptures":[31]

> The Lord bless thee, and keep thee:
> The Lord make his face shine upon thee, and be gracious
>   unto thee:
> The Lord lift up his countenance upon thee, and give thee
>   peace. (6:24-26)

The narrative portions of the book are told with the same vigor and enthusiasm that we see in Genesis and Exodus. Most of the narratives are short—accounts of mere incidents—but taken all together, they make up a memorable though episodic history of almost forty years of passage through a wasteland, a passage altogether so painful and discouraging that the people repeatedly "murmur" against their leaders and almost lose faith in God. Only the stalwart leadership of Moses is able to stifle rebellion and persuade the people to persevere till they can reach the Promised Land.

The book falls into three logical divisions: (1) preparations to leave Mount Sinai (1:1–10:10); (2) the wandering in the wilderness (10:11–19:22); and (3) the events of the last year before reaching Canaan (20:1–36:13).[32]

Preparations for the Journey (1:1–10:10). God commands Moses to take a census of the twelve tribes. The total number of the people "from twenty years old and upward, all that were able to go to war" is 603,550. The Levites, the women, and the children are not counted in this number. After offerings by all the princes (tribal leaders), the people are ready to set out on their journey.

Wandering in the Wilderness (10:11–19:22). The story of the sojourn in the wilderness is principally one of grumbling and dissatisfaction on the part of the people. They continually find fault with Moses and are even ungrateful for the Lord's providence. This period of wandering is of immense significance to Hebrew tradition. It is referred to countless times by later Biblical historians, by the Psalmists, and by the prophets. Sometimes (as in Hosea 11:1-5) it is regarded as a sort of childhood of the nation, a training period, an age of innocence. Nearly always it is pointed out as an era when God was especially protective and provident.

QUAILS AND PLAGUE (11:1-33). Although manna still falls every night, the people yearn for the meat and the fish, the cucumbers and the melons, the onions and the garlic to which they have been accustomed in Egypt. They complain so loudly that Moses takes the problem to God. Angry at their complaints, God promises to send them enough meat to last a whole month—so much that it will come out of their nostrils! A wind blows to the people a great multitude of quails, which fall and cover the earth. When the people eat, a terrible plague smites them so that many die.

SEDITION OF MIRIAM AND AARON (12:1-15). Even the brother and the sister of Moses become disaffected and resent their brother's authority. "Hath the Lord indeed spoken only by Moses? hath he not spoken also by us?" Again the Lord is displeased. This time he afflicts Miriam with leprosy. Then Aaron repents, while Moses prays to God that Miriam may be cured; after seven days of the punishment she is made well again.

RECONNAISSANCE OF CANAAN (13:1-14:35). Next Moses sends out twelve spies, one from each tribe, to reconnoiter the Promised Land of Canaan. On their return, ten of the spies report that the land is indeed flowing with milk and honey, but that it is inhabited by men of great stature and even by giants, "the sons of Anak," in whose sight the Israelites would be as mere grasshoppers. Caleb and Joshua, the other two spies, dissent from the majority report and urge invasion of the land. Agreeing with the ten spies, the people again murmur and weep and wish that they had died in Egypt; once more the Lord becomes angry and, in spite of Moses' entreaties, decrees that the murmurers shall never enter the Promised Land.

The Last Year of the Journey (20:1-36:13). As the years roll slowly on, little progress toward Canaan is made by the still-murmuring Hebrews. Miriam dies in Kadesh and is buried there (20:1). Aaron dies upon Mount Hor and is succeeded by his son Eleazar (20:22-29); even Moses loses his right to enter the Promised Land.

STRIKING OF THE ROCK (20:2-13).* In a period of serious drought the people again wish that they had died earlier. Moses and Aaron ask God for water and are told to *speak to* a particular rock and that it will give enough water for the people and their animals. Moses, who has formerly interceded for the people, now loses his patience: "Hear now, ye rebels; must we fetch you water out of this rock?" And instead of speaking to the

---

* One should remember that this is the second rock-striking episode told of Moses (the other is in Ex. 17:1-7). Biblical scholars feel reasonably sure that the compilers of the Hexateuch used different sources containing two versions of the same event and for one reason or another did not conflate the two accounts. One Rabbinical explanation of the second striking is that the rock which Moses struck according to Exodus followed the Israelites in their journey across the wilderness—an explanation accepted by St. Paul, who augments the ancient tradition by identifying the rock with Christ (I Cor. 10:4).

rock, he strikes it with his rod. Water gushes forth in great plenty. God says that Moses and Aaron will be punished for their disobedience by not being allowed to enter Canaan.*

THE FIERY SERPENTS (21:4-9). The people are incurably rebellious. When they murmur again, God sends a plague of fiery serpents upon them. Again Moses intercedes for the people, and the Lord tells him to make a brass serpent and put it on a pole; anybody bitten by one of the live snakes may be cured by looking at Moses' brazen one.

BALAAM AND HIS ASS (22:1–24:25). Indubitably the finest literary gem in the book of Numbers is the story of Balaam. Apprised of the victories which the Israelites have won over the Amorites, Balak, king of the Moabites, fears this multitude which has come out of Egypt. Desiring to lay a curse upon the Israelites, he sends for the prophet Balaam, "a transitional figure between the primitive soothsayer and the type of moral prophet, unique among the Hebrews. . . ." [33] Now, Balaam is a worshiper of the Lord, and he asks the Lord for guidance in the matter. God at first refuses but later agrees to allow Balaam to go to Balak. When Balaam sets out on his ass, God sends an angel to block the way. Only the ass, however, can see the angel with "his sword drawn in his hand." When Balaam repeatedly urges the animal forward, it turns first aside, then crushes its master's foot against a wall, and finally falls down. Balaam strikes the ass with his staff, whereupon God allows the beast to speak: "What have I done unto thee, that thou hast smitten me these three times?" At last Balaam's eyes are opened; he sees the angel, realizes that the Israelites have God on their side, begs God's forgiveness, and is allowed to proceed on his journey to meet Balak. When the king asks the prophet to curse the Israelites, Balaam refuses and delivers four poetic oracles of great literary excellence (23:7-10, 23:18-24, 24:3-9, and 24:15-24). In these he praises the Israelites as God's Chosen People and predicts their future greatness as a nation.

We learn eventually (31:8) that Balaam is slain in battle as the Hebrews advance victoriously against the Moabites and the Midianites.

* The cause of God's punishment of Moses and Aaron is a matter of dispute. Numbers 20:12 says that the offense is "unbelief," but 20:24 says that it is "rebellion."

THE SECOND CENSUS (26:1-65). Encamped on the plains of Moab, the Hebrew people are again counted. Although the various plagues and also God's decision not to allow any of those who left Egypt (except Caleb and Joshua) to enter the Promised Land tend to limit the Hebrew migrants to Canaan, the number of fighting men available there reaches the substantial total of 601,730.

THE END OF THE JOURNEY (Chs. 27–36). As they stand beside the river Jordan, the descendants of Israel reach important decisions. The tribes of Reuben and Gad choose to remain on the east bank of the Jordan. Forty-eight cities are given to the Levites; six of these are set aside as places of refuge for those who have unintentionally committed homicide.* Joshua is appointed successor to Moses.

DEUTERONOMY

The name of the fifth book of the Hexateuch is of Greek origin and means "second law." It refers to the repetition by Moses of the religious and ethical code which he enjoins the people to obey.

The nucleus of the book of Deuteronomy (Chs. 5–26 and 28) is believed to be identical with the book of law discovered in the Temple at Jerusalem in 621 B.C., during the reign of Josiah.† It seems likely that all but a few chapters (added by later editors) were the work of a priest or prophet of the kingdom of Judah and that he wrote the book during the reign of Manasseh, the predecessor of Amon and Josiah. This author is known as "the Deuteronomist."

Manasseh had been a wicked king. He had let the Temple in Jerusalem fall into disrepair, he had turned to the worship of other gods than the Lord, and he had even burned his own son as a sacrificial offering (see II Kings 21). The Deuteronomist was eager to restore the people of Judah to the religious practices traditionally believed to have been handed down by Moses.

---

* The brutal customs of the time are reflected in the accounts of how the Hebrews conquer the Midianites, burn their cities, kill all the men (31:7) and capture the women and children. Moses objects to sparing the women; he orders the killing of all mature women and male children, but allows the girls to be kept as slaves.

† See the discussion of the D Document on p. 45.

He emphasized God's goodness and love and the necessity of worshiping him and him alone.

"The author must have been a man of strong feeling, abundant imagination, and a disciplined mind, for he has transformed law into literature and made legal statutes flame with spiritual passion. . . . In this book we have something unique: law flaming with personality, the spirit of the law speaking in the cadences of great music, statutes luminous with spiritual passion. Law has become literature, the literature of power." [34]

Deuteronomy is essentially a restatement of the Mosaic law. But there is a considerable difference between this lawgiving and most of the juridic writings in the Old Testament: Deuteronomy is addressed not to the priests, the kings, or the judges, but to the laity. Instead of being concerned principally with ceremonies and rituals, it treats many matters of daily conduct: the religious education of children (6:20-25); sacrifices (12:5-14); food (12: 15-28 and 14:3-21); tithes (14:22-29); the relief of poverty (15: 4-11); the treatment of slaves and servants (15:12-18); the observance of festivals (16:1-17); lying witnesses (19:16-19); the inheritance of first-born sons of two wives (21:15); the punishment of a rebellious son by stoning him to death (21:18-21); sexual purity (22:13-30); divorces (24:1-4); loans and pledges (24:10-13); humanity to culprits—the famous limiting of a flogging to forty stripes lest "thy brother should seem vile unto thee" (25:1-3); proper treatment of animals at work (25:4); and many others. (As noted above, the oft-quoted law of revenge, "life shall go for life, eye for eye, tooth for tooth . . . " [19:21] was not strictly enforced but was interpreted as a plea for equitable, proportionate justice as in requiring adequate, but not excessive, compensation for serious injury.) It is the spiritual satisfaction derived from the keeping of such laws that enables Psalmists to exult with such outbursts as "O how love I thy law! it is my meditation all the day" (Psalms 119:97) and "Thy word is a lamp unto my feet, and a light unto my path" (Psalms 119:105). And it was Christ's violation of some of these laws that made the Pharisees hostile to Christianity.

The book of Deuteronomy consists chiefly of three addresses and two poems, all attributed to Moses. Bits of narrative are interspersed among these five main divisions, and the book ends with an account of the death of Moses.

The First Address (1:1–4:40). In his first speech Moses gives a brief review of all that has happened to the Israelites since their departure from Horeb (Mount Sinai). He stresses the fact that God has kept his half of the Covenant and urges the Israelites to keep theirs by obeying God's laws.

The Second Address (5:1–26:19). This address makes up the bulk of the book. Here are repeated the Ten Commandments (5:6-21) and other laws, known as the "Covenant Code" (Chs. 12–28). "The emphasis is on justice and righteousness as it applies to both the private and the collective life of the people of Israel." [35] In this address there is a prediction (18:15-22) that God will send to Israel a prophet into whose mouth God will

---

THE FOUR CODES OF THE PENTATEUCH [36]

Four principal collections of legislation appear in the Pentateuch. Some of the individual laws may have originated as early as the days of Moses; the collection or codification, however, was much later.

1. *The Covenant Code* (Ex. 20–23) is regarded as the oldest body of Hebrew law, and it reflects an agricultural society. Its name is derived from the Covenant between God and the Israelites, the promise of God to prosper them provided they kept these laws. This code may be dated between 900 and 650 B.C.

2. *The Deuteronomic Code* (Deut. 12–28) reflects a more humanitarian spirit and a nobler concept of God than does the Covenant Code. Here God is universal and more loving, and he expects man to be merciful and generous. This code insists, too, on centralization of worship, especially in Jerusalem. The code is generally dated 621 B.C.

3. *The Holiness Code* (Lev. 17–26) emphasizes ritual, but lays some stress, too, on personal and social ethics. Some scholars consider the code post-Exilic (that is, later than 536 B.C.); others think it originated about a century before that date.

4. *The Priestly Code* (scattered through Exodus, Leviticus, and Numbers) emphasizes ceremonialism, cult, and ritual as deemed especially significant by the priests and scribes in Jerusalem after the Hebrews' return from the Babylonian Captivity. Most scholars date these priestly laws about 400 B.C.

put his commandments. It seems likely that the Deuteronomist is here justifying the important role of the prophets of the eighth and seventh centuries; and this passage may have had a great deal to do with the growth of the messianic hope of the Hebrews.

The Third Address (29:1–31:6). In short speeches (Chapters 27, 28) * Moses lists the blessings which will be bestowed on the people if they obey God's law and also the dire consequences if they disobey. Again he reminds them of the Covenant and tells them that their future is in their own hands: they have the freedom to choose whether or not they will earn the blessings which God has promised. "Choice is a perilous gift. Morality is a matter of choice. Without morality life is not attainable and the result is death." [37] "See, I have set before thee this day life and good, and death and evil" (30:15).

The Last Song of Moses (32:1-43). After delivering his final warning to the people, Moses bursts into song, glorifying God and praising his justice and his goodness:

> He is the Rock, his work is perfect:
> For all his ways are judgment:
> A God of truth and without iniquity,
> Just and right is he. (32:4)

The song reviews how God has brought Israel safely through many tribulations:

> He found him [Israel] in a desert land,
> And in the waste howling wilderness;
> He led him about,
> He instructed him,
> He kept him as the apple of his eye. (32:10)

But Israel has provoked God to anger by worshiping strange deities and sacrificing to devils. God therefore has punished Israel by allowing other nations to mistreat it. Now it has repented of its sins, and God will avenge the suffering of his Chosen People. (This portion suggests that The Last Song of Moses is of Exilic or post-Exilic origin.)

---

* Chapter 27, believed to be an interpolation by some Exilic or post-Exilic editor, is a disjointed chapter consisting of (1) exhortations and precepts put into the mouth of Moses and (2) a series of curses upon those who disobey certain laws.

The Blessing of Moses (33:1-29). This poem is reminiscent of Jacob's blessing (Gen. 49:2-27); but, unlike the other poem, it "idealizes its subjects" [38] instead of detailing the characteristics of each tribe. It barely mentions Judah and Reuben, or Dan and Naphtali, and it fails to mention Simeon at all. The tribe of Levi and the two tribes descended from Joseph (Ephraim and Manasseh) receive the most attention. Though literarily inferior to The Last Song of Moses, the Blessing is, nevertheless, a noble and majestic poem. It contains many such striking figures as these:

> And the Lord shall cover him [Benjamin] all the day long,
> And he shall dwell between his shoulders. (33:12)

> His [Joseph's] glory is like the firstling of his bullock,
> And his horns are like the horns of unicorns:
> With them he shall push the people together
> To the ends of the earth. (33:17)

And finally these immortal lines:

> The eternal God is thy refuge,
> And underneath are the everlasting arms . . . (33:27)

The Death of Moses (34:1-12). The Pentateuch closes appropriately with the death of its greatest figure, the faithful and indomitable lawgiver, who has now led the wayward children of Israel to the boundary between Moab and Canaan. His work is finished. Alone he walks to the top of Mount Nebo. From there God shows him the Promised Land, which he has been forbidden to enter. So Moses, the Lord's servant, dies in the land of Moab.

JOSHUA

The last book of the Hexateuch is named for its leading character; the Hebrew proper name means "the Lord saves."

The book of Joshua is an idealized and "schematized" [39] history of the Israelites' conquest and division of Canaan. It covers a period of about twenty-five years, beginning at a point shortly after the death of Moses. This history gives the impression that virtually all the tribes were united under the command of Joshua, that the conquest was steadily progressive, and that except for a few spots Canaan was conquered by the end of the twenty-five-year period. This impression is contradicted by the account of the same period contained in the first chapter of Judges. The book of Joshua seems to be a neat but somewhat misleading re-arrangement by the Deuteronomist and the priestly editors of events which took place over more than a century. Archeological excavations indicate that there *was* a series of battles and de-structions of cities in Palestine at the end of the thirteenth century B.C. and later.

The book is not altogether a pleasant one. It is too bloody and full of merciless destruction to appeal to modern taste. Its titular hero has the virtues of courage, singleness of purpose, persever-ance, and obedience to God; but he is cruel and revengeful, and he lacks the grandeur and the vision of Moses. The God of Joshua is depicted as "a God of war, revenge, and bloodshed, who hates the enemies of Israel with merciless and bitter hatred. . . . This is primitive religion at its worst." [40]

The purpose of the book is twofold: first, to demonstrate how God has kept his promise to his Chosen People as long as they obeyed his commandments; and second, to make Joshua appear a hero and a worthy successor to Moses.

The book has three main parts: (1) the conquest of Canaan (Chs. 1–12); (2) division of the conquered territory (Chs. 13–22); and (3) Joshua's farewell address and his death (Chs. 23–24).

The Conquest of Canaan (Chs. 1–12). The first twelve chapters tell of Israel's crossing of the Jordan River (the waters are mirac-ulously dammed so that the people cross the river on dry ground) and of the subduing of most of western Palestine about 1200 B.C. Although the account contains much bloodshed and cruelty, it is an orderly and spirited tale told with great enthusiasm. Sev-eral episodes deserve special notice.

RAHAB AND THE SPIES (2:1-22 and 6:22-25). The important city of Jericho lies athwart the intended route of the Israelites; it must be captured if the campaign is to succeed. Having been a spy himself, Joshua knows the value of espionage and so sends two men into Jericho to "view the land." They find lodging at the house of Rahab, a harlot, who tells them that the inhabi-tants of Jericho are faint with terror at the approach of Israel. She says that the Israelites' earlier victories have convinced her that their God is indeed the God of heaven and earth. Therefore she turns traitor to her own people and hides the spies when a searching party sent by the king of Jericho comes to find them.

After exacting a promise that she and her family will be protected when the city falls, she lets the spies down over the wall of the city by means of a "scarlet cord"; this cord is to mark her house when Israel enters Jericho. Later, when the city does fall to the conquerors, Rahab and all her kindred are spared, and she is allowed to live out her days in her native land.

THE FALL OF JERICHO (6:1-27). As the Hebrews' army approaches Jericho, the city shuts itself up within its walls and prepares to withstand a siege. In obedience to the directions of the Lord, Joshua proceeds in the following manner: a great procession marches around the city once every day for six days. First comes the main body of the soldiers—"mighty men of valor"; next are seven priests, who blow continually on trumpets of rams' horns; after these come some more priests bearing the Ark of the Covenant; finally, a rear guard follows the Ark. On the seventh day the procession marches around Jericho seven times, the priests blowing the trumpets all the while. Then Joshua says to the people: "Shout; for the Lord hath given you the city!" And the people shout with a great shout, and the walls fall down flat, so that the people go up into the city, every man straight before him, and they take the city. Except for Rahab and her kinsmen, every living thing in the city is destroyed, "both man and woman, young and old, and ox, and sheep, and ass, with the edge of the sword." * Joshua pronounces a curse against anyone who should ever rebuild the city.

THE SIN OF ACHAN (7:1-26). After Jericho the next obstacle in the path of Israel is the small city of Ai. Joshua sends an expeditionary force of three thousand to take the city; but they are repulsed and some of them are slain. When Joshua cries out to God in grief and despair, God tells him that the defeat is punishment for a sin committed by some Israelite. Investigation reveals that Achan has appropriated for his own use a garment, some silver, and some gold—all from the spoils of Jericho.

---

* Archeological excavations have demonstrated that the walls of Jericho did fall. Scholars have suggested that one may suppose, "without minimizing the divine guidance of events," that the physical cause of the collapse of the walls was an earthquake. See John Bright, exegesis to Joshua, *The Interpreter's Bible*, II, 581-582. The account in Joshua is an excellent illustration of how Old Testament historians could incorporate into their narratives such actual facts as the mysterious ruins of a city—whether their purpose was to substantiate the legends or merely to account for the facts.

Joshua orders Achan and all his family and possessions, including the stolen spoils, to be brought into the valley of Achor.
There the culprit and his family are stoned and their bodies
burned. "So the Lord turned from the fierceness of his anger."

THE DESTRUCTION OF AI (8:1-29). Now Joshua employs a
stratagem to overcome Ai. He sends his main force of thirty
thousand to lie in ambush on the west of the city. Next he leads
an attack from the north. When the defenders of Ai come out
in a mass, the Israelites on the north retreat, and their enemies
pursue them. Then the soldiers in ambush rush in, capture the
city, and burn it. Twelve thousand of its inhabitants are killed.
The king, who has been taken captive, is hanged. The "cattle
and spoil" of the city are appropriated by the Israelites.

THE WILES OF THE GIBEONITES (9:1-27). Fearing the might
and the cruelty of Joshua's men, the inhabitants of Gibeon send
to Joshua envoys who (by displaying to him worn-out shoes and
clothes, patched wineskins, and moldy bread) pretend that they
have come from a distant land. Joshua makes a peace pact with
them. When he discovers that they are in reality close neighbors, he decrees that thenceforth the Gibeonites must be the
servants of the Israelites—"hewers of wood and drawers of water."

THE BATTLE OF GIBEON (10:1-27). Five kings of the Amorites
now join forces to oppose Joshua. They attack him at Gibeon,
but the Lord comes to the aid of his people. The Israelites begin
to gain the upper hand, yet Joshua fears that daylight will fail
before his victory is complete. Therefore he prays to the Lord
and speaks the famous words:

> Sun, stand thou still upon Gibeon;
> And thou, Moon, in the valley of Ajalon. (10:12)

The Lord answers his prayers, and the sun and the moon remain
motionless till the enemies of Israel are routed. To add to the
Amorites' troubles, God sends great hailstones, which kill more
men than do the Israelites. The five kings flee and hide in a
cave. When Joshua is told of their hiding place, he orders the
mouth of the cave to be closed with great stones; and he commands his men to pursue the Amorites so that they cannot re-
enter their city. After the great slaughter is ended, the five kings
are brought from the cave; they are killed and their bodies are
hanged for display.

THE END OF THE CAMPAIGN (10:28–12:24). Joshua's men fight many other battles, two of the most famous being those at the waters of Merom and at Hazor. All enemies are defeated, even the giant race of Anakim to whom (Nu. 13:33) the Israelites are "as grasshoppers." Altogether, thirty-one kings and their armies are vanquished (including those at Jericho). Although large areas (such as the land of the Philistines in the southwest) remain unconquered, Joshua decides that it is time to divide the country among the tribes that have crossed the Jordan.

The Division of Canaan (Chs. 13–22). The ten chapters devoted to the assigning of land to each tribe repeat much of the material found in Exodus and Deuteronomy, and they contain much methodical listing of cities, rivers, and families. This is the sort of writing which was especially dear to the priestly authors, but which the modern student of literature is inclined to skip.

Joshua's Farewell Address and His Death (Chs. 23–24). Joshua is now "old and stricken in age." Like Moses, he calls all the Israelites together to hear his final exhortations. He points out the great blessings which the Lord has showered upon them. He urges them "to do all that is written in the book of the law of Moses." Fearing that they might be tempted to worship the gods of the Canaanites, he warns his people that the Lord "is an holy God; he is a jealous God; he will not forgive your transgressions nor your sins." The people promise to serve the Lord and obey his voice.

Joshua dies and is buried on Mount Ephraim.

4

Rise and Fall of the Monarchy
(From Judges to the Exile)

After the death of Joshua, as the need for a strong central government in Israel became clear, the monarchy was established under Saul. The history of the Hebrew people from the period before Saul until the time of the Exile in 586 B.C. is related in Judges, I and II Samuel, and I and II Kings.

JUDGES: TREND TOWARD NATIONAL UNITY AND SECULAR GOVERNMENT

This book derives its name from the title given to the leaders of various groups of Israelites before the establishment of the monarchy under Saul. Although called "judges," these dignitaries usually served at one and the same time as military and religious leaders and as civil magistrates.

It is believed that the composition of the book of Judges went through the following stages: [1] (1) Between 1200 and 900 B.C. historical stories and legends developed, many of them in the form of narrative poems. (2) These were transmitted orally for a few centuries, and then they were converted into prose tales, possibly by the authors of the J and E documents.* (3) At some time during the eighth or the seventh century B.C., an unidentified editor (possibly the one who conflated the J and E documents) combined the separate tales into a continuous narrative. (4) The Deuteronomist † re-edited most of the material now making up Judges 2:6–16:31, probably about 621 B.C. (5) In the latter part

* See above, pp. 44-46, the discussion of the growth of the Hexateuch.

† See above, pp. 45 and 71-75, the discussion of the D Document and the book of Deuteronomy.

of the sixth century B.C., after the Exile, some unknown editor added the introduction (1:1–2:5), the "appendixes" (17:1–21:25), and possibly 3:31 and 9:1-57.

The book of Joshua leaves the impression that by the time of the death of the titular hero, the Hebrew tribes had pretty well subdued most of Canaan and had organized themselves into a united nation under one leader. The book of Judges, on the contrary, gives a picture of the tribes frequently squabbling with each other and continually fighting against their non-Hebrew neighbors. Biblical scholars are inclined to believe that Judges gives the more accurate account.

The book is not, however, an entirely reliable history. Much of its material belongs to the realm of folklore: the chronology is confused; and many of the tales are colored by the editors' desire to point a moral.

The three main parts of the book are: (1) the introduction (1:1–2:5); (2) a cycle of stories about the lives and the times of the twelve (or thirteen if "King" Abimelech is counted) judges who presided over some of the Israelites after the death of Joshua (2:6–16:31), and (3) the two appendixes, concerned respectively with the migration of the Danites (17–18) and the offense of Gibeah (19–21).

Post-Exilic Introduction to the Book (1:1–2:5). The first portion of the book of Judges is an attempt by the post-Exilic editor to furnish a transition between the book of Joshua and the Deuteronomist's tales of the twelve judges. It tells of several conquests in the land of Canaan, some of which have already been related in the book of Joshua.

Tales about the Judges (2:6–16:31). The longest and by far the most significant portion of the book deals with the adventures of the judges themselves. This section uses a review of the funeral of Joshua to emphasize the fact that a new era began soon after the death of that hero. Next, the cycle of stories about the judges is set into a sort of didactic framework: each story is made to illustrate the Deuteronomist's favorite thesis: that God is just and will punish his people when they sin against him, but is merciful and will send aid when they are obedient or repent and beg for deliverance. Every story is introduced by an almost stereotyped formula: "And the children of Israel did evil in the sight of the Lord. . . . And the anger of the Lord was hot against Israel, and

he delivered them into the hands of spoilers that spoiled them. . . .
But when the children of Israel cried unto the Lord, the Lord
raised up a deliverer . . . " [2] In each case the deliverer is one of
the judges.

These judges and the passages which tell of their exploits are
designated in the following table:

    (1) Othniel (1:11-13; 3:7-11).
    (2) Ehud (3:12-30).
    (3) Shamgar (3:31).
    (4) Deborah (4—5).
    (5) Gideon (6:1—8:32).
    (6) (Perhaps) Abimelech (8:33—9:57).
    (7) Tola (10:1-2).
    (8) Jair (10:3-5).
    (9) Jephthah (10:6—12:7).
    (10) Ibzan (12:8-10).
    (11) Elon (12:11-12).
    (12) Abdon (12:13-15).
    (13) Samson (13—16).

Of this number, Shamgar, Tola, Jair, Ibzan, Elon, and Abdon are
sometimes known as the "minor" judges. Abimelech is called a
"king," (9:6); some commentators, however, include him in the
list of judges.

OTHNIEL (1:11-13; 3:7-11). Othniel, the first of the twelve
judges, is renowned for his military expoits (he captures Debir,
receiving Caleb's daughter for his wife as a reward, and later
rescues the Israelites from a neighboring king).

EHUD THE TYRANNICIDE (3:12-30). Once when the people do
evil, they are forced by God to serve Eglon, King of Moab, for
eighteen years. Then Ehud, chosen to deliver Israel's tribute to
Eglon, conceals a two-edged dagger beneath his clothes and deceives Eglon by pretending that he has a secret which nobody
but the king must hear. Ehud says: "I have a message from God
unto thee." Now, "Eglon was a very fat man. . . . And Ehud put
forth his left hand, and took the dagger from his right thigh, and
thrust it into his belly; and the haft also went in after the blade;
and the fat closed upon the blade, so that he could not draw the
dagger out of his belly; and the dirt came out." After so daring a
feat, Ehud rallies the Israelites and leads them in a victorious
battle against Moab.

DEBORAH THE PROPHETESS (Chs. 4—5). Far more renowned than Ehud is Deborah, prophetess and judge, whose religious fervor and "flaming patriotism" [3] inspire the soldier Barak to lead Israel's army against the Canaanitish host under the command of Sisera. Now the Israelites have been cruelly oppressed by Canaan for twenty years. Deborah convinces Barak that the Lord will give his people victory over Sisera on Mount Tabor, by the river Kishon, where Sisera's "nine hundred chariots of iron" will be ineffective. A battle takes place, and Deborah's prophecy is fulfilled: all of Sisera's men are killed, and Sisera himself finds refuge in the tent of a Hebrew woman named Jael, who pretends friendship but kills him while he sleeps.

These events, related in unadorned prose in Chapter 4, become the subject of a brilliant victory song in Chapter 5, known as the "Song of Deborah and Barak." *

There is no other poem in Hebrew literature, whether early or late, which displays such seemingly unconscious and spontaneous literary art. The intense patriotic and religious passion of its writer flames in every line, sweeping on and up to the dramatic climax. It is throughout both an ancient *Te Deum* in praise of the God of Israel and a superb account of a mighty contest in which not only kings fought, but the stars of heaven and a river in its divinely swollen course. . . . Nothing is finer in the annals of war of any literature than this, nor has it been excelled in imagination or in expression by any of the later war poems of Israel.[4]

Exclusive of a brief introduction and a final curse, the poem may be divided into three main parts. The first part (5:4-11) describes the terrifying approach of God himself toward the battlefield: the earth trembles and the mountains melt. Then there is a picture of the villages and highways, which have long been left desolate for fear of the Canaanites. The second section (5: 12-18) opens with a plea to Deborah and Barak to arise, sing, and lead on to victory. Next comes a series of praises for those tribes which respond to Barak's appeal for mobilization—Ephraim, Benjamin, Machir (Manasseh), Issachar, and Naphthali. The author voices his (or her) contempt for the cowardly tribes of Gilead (Gad), Reuben, Asher, and Dan, who have refused

* It is believed that this song is (with the possible exception of part of the Song of Moses and the People [Exodus 15:1]) the oldest part of the Bible, to be dated 1150-1100 B.C.

to join in the battle. The third and most ecstatic part of the ode (5:19-31) begins with a litotes full of grim and exultant humor: *

> The kings came and fought;
> Then fought the kings of Canaan,
> In Taanach by the waters of Megiddo;
> They took no gain of money.

The Israelites are aided by the natural forces:

> They fought from heaven.
> The stars in their courses fought against Sisera.
> The river of Kishon swept them away,
> That ancient river, the river Kishon.

The climax of the whole story is the slaying of Sisera. Wearied beyond endurance and fearful for his life, he asks Jael for shelter and protection. She calms his fears by bringing him better refreshment than he requests:

> He asked water, and she gave him milk;
> She brought forth butter in a lordly dish.

When he falls asleep, she seizes a nail (or tent peg) and with a hammer drives it through both his temples. The poetess gloats over the scene which she imagines must be taking place at Sisera's home:

> The mother of Sisera looked out at a window,
> And cried through the lattice,
> "Why is his chariot so long in coming?
> Why tarry the wheels of his chariots?"

The ladies in waiting assure Sisera's mother that her son is only gathering up the spoils of battle.

Without offering any transition, the poetess then ends the ode abruptly:

> So let all Thine enemies perish, O Lord:
> But let them that love him be as the sun
> When he goeth forth in his might.

GIDEON THE SHREWD (6:1—8:32). The tale of Gideon is an exciting and melodramatic tale. About 1100 B.C. the Midianites, Amalekites, and other "children of the east" were continually

---

* Compare the many litotes in *Beowulf.*

making predatory raids on Israelite settlements. The number of these predators was so great that the historian likens them to swarms of grasshoppers or locusts. The Hebrews are now confronted with a new "secret weapon" *—the camel (this attack by the Midianites has been called the first camel raid in recorded history [5]). Once again, as in the days of Deborah, normal agricultural activity among the Israelites is almost at a standstill. The Lord calls upon Gideon, the youngest son of a poor farmer, to deliver his people. Gideon begins his work for the Lord by destroying his father's altar to Baal and the grove beside it (6:25-27). He has misgivings about his abilities as a soldier, but when the Lord promises him aid and reassures him by giving him three miraculous signs, Gideon agrees to undertake the mission. Thirty-two thousand men flock to his standards, but only 10,000 remain when the leader sends home all who admit to being afraid. The number is still far too great, for the Lord wants the Israelites to know that it is the divine might and not the power of the people which will overcome Midian. The number is therefore reduced by a test: the men are all led to the water and told to drink. All who throw themselves on their knees to drink are judged insufficiently vigilant and alert; the three hundred who drink from their hands are chosen.

Now Gideon plans a surprise attack by night. He gives each man a torch (concealed in a pitcher) and a trumpet. This group then surrounds the Midianite camp. In the dead of night at a signal from Gideon, all three hundred wave the torches on high, break the pitchers (to sound like the clashing of armor), blow on the trumpets, and cry out: "The sword of the Lord, and of Gideon!" Believing themselves surrounded by a mighty army, the Midianites flee in panic, and the Lord sets "every man's sword against his fellow." The rout is complete. The next day the Ephraimites aid in "mopping up." Never again are the Israelites molested by the robbers of Midian.

The picture of Gideon is a rather attractive one. To be sure, he is cruel and sometimes vengeful: he captures and executes the two princes and the two kings of the Midianites, and he punishes the elders of Succoth (for their refusal to feed his

---

* The Hebrews are continually having to fight against superior weapons (for example, the iron chariots of the Canaanites as recorded in Judges 4:13).

army) by tearing their flesh with thorns and briers. But he is a humble servant of God, not at all ambitious or eager for personal glory; witness his refusal to be made king (8:22-23). Furthermore, he is a shrewd general, and he is very human in his early fear of the Midianites, his requiring of miraculous signs from God, his yearning for the earrings of the slain foe, and his self-indulgence during his latter years (he has seventy sons by "many wives" and also an illegitimate son, Abimelech).

"KING" ABIMELECH (8:33—9:57). Son of Gideon and a concubine from the city of Shechem, the cruel and treacherous Abimelech murders all his legitimate half-brothers except Jotham who escapes death by going into hiding. Then he is made king by the men of Shechem. Somewhat later his subjects revolt and are ruthlessly destroyed. While besieging an enemy city, Abimelech himself is grievously wounded by a woman who fractures his skull with a piece of millstone; he orders one of his soldiers to slay him so that posterity will not say that he was killed by a woman.

Of greater literary interest than the story of Abimelech itself is the famous Fable of Jotham (9:7-21), one of the rare instances of this type of folklore in the Bible.[*] When Abimelech is made king, Jotham (from a safe distance—"on the top of Mount Gerizim") tells how the bramble accepted the position as king of trees after the olive tree, the fig tree, and the vine all had refused the offer of the crown. The bramble then warned the trees that if they were disloyal, he, the bramble, would destroy them all with fire. Jotham is, of course, pointing out to the Shechemites that they have chosen a wicked and dangerous sovereign, and he prophesies that Abimelech and his subjects will destroy each other.

JEPHTHAH THE RASH (10:6—12:7). The piteous tale of Jephthah and his daughter has always been a favorite with modern readers. It contains several elements which appear in the traditional literature of many nations: (1) "the rise to power of a banished hero";[6] (2) the rash vow, especially a vow to sacrifice some-

---

[*] The Bible contains many parables but few fables. Both of these genres are short tales which illustrate some truth or moral principle. The fable, however, is in a lighter vein and on a lower ethical plane than the parable and unlike the parable usually contains some impossible phenomenon, such as the talking of animals, whereas the parable contains no such phenomenon. Another instance of the fable in the Bible is that of the body and its members (I Cor. 12:14-26).

thing; and (3) the lament of a maiden for her virginity (that is, a maiden's lament over the fact that she is about to die before she has experienced marriage and motherhood).*

Jephthah, of humble birth (he is the son of a harlot), is driven from his native land (Gilead) into the land of Tob. When oppressed by the Ammonites, the Gileadites recall Jephthah and make him their leader. He vows to God that if he is victorious, he will sacrifice as a burnt offering whoever comes first out of his house to meet him on his return. He subdues the Ammonites, and his only daughter (whose name is never mentioned) comes out to greet him "with timbrels and with dances." Deep is his grief, but after an interval of two months (during which time she dwells in the mountains and bemoans her virginity), he carries out his vow. Each year thereafter the women of Gilead spend four days lamenting the daughter of Jephthah.

SAMSON THE MIGHTY (Chs. 13–16). It is generally agreed that the stories of Samson constitute the literary masterpiece of the book of Judges. Their central figure is not only a typical legendary strong man but also a tragic hero.

The accounts of Samson's exploits have several earmarks of folklore—exaggeration, practical joking, posing of riddles, and broad, boisterous humor. Killing a thousand Philistines with the jawbone of an ass, catching three hundred foxes and tying torches to their tails in order to burn his enemies' grain fields, pulling down a temple with his bare hands—such feats compare with the mighty deeds of Hercules in Greek legends, of Thor in Norse mythology, and of Paul Bunyan in American loggers' yarns.

If great physical strength and a penchant for practical joking were the only characteristics of Samson, then he would not be especially heroic; but his is the story of a devout and valorous man, who, chosen by God to deliver the Israelites from the Philistines, suffers ignominy and death at the hands of the cruel enemy. Consequently his downfall has inspired the creation of many noble works of art, notably Milton's *Samson Agonistes*, Handel's *Samson*, and Saint-Saens's *Samson and Delilah*.

This is Samson's story as told in the book of Judges:

An angel appears unto the wife of one Manoah and tells her that she is going to conceive and bear a son,† who will deliver

---

* Compare Iphigenia's lament in Euripides' *Iphigenia at Aulis* and Antigone's lament in Sophocles' *Antigone*.

† See note, p. 51, above.

PALESTINE
THE PERIOD
OF THE JUDGES

SCALE OF MILES
0   5   30

KNOWN BOUNDARIES
PROBABLE BOUNDARIES

The Great Sea

Tyre
Accho
Dor
Megiddo
Joppa
Ashdod
Ashkelon
Gaza
Beer-sheba

MT. CARMEL
Sea of Chinnereth
Nazareth

ASHER
NAPHTALI
ZEBULUN
ISSACHAR
BASHAN
MANASSEH
MANASSEH
EPHRAIM
Shiloh
Bethel
DAN
Jericho
BENJAMIN
Jerusalem
Bethlehem
JUDAH
Hebron
SIMEON
GAD
AMMON
REUBEN
MOAB

Jordan River
River Jordan
Salt Sea

PHILISTINES

SEIR
EDOM

From A *Handbook for Know Your Bible Study Groups*, © 1959 by Abingdon Press. By permission of the publisher.

the Israelites from the Philistines, the current scourge of God's people. The angel warns her against ever shaving the boy's hair. In due time Samson is born, grows into manhood, and soon manifests prodigious strength.

His first feat is the slaying of a lion with his bare hands. This he accomplishes en route to visit an unnamed Philistine woman. On his return he notices a swarm of bees and some honey in the carcass of the lion. This suggests to Samson a riddle, which he later poses to thirty Philistine men: "Out of the eater came forth meat, and out of the strong came forth sweetness." He wagers a "change of garments" with each that none of them can solve the riddle. His sweetheart wheedles the answer from him and divulges it to her countrymen. And wrathful Samson smites "thirty men of them" (other Philistines) and uses their clothing to pay off his wager.

Samson's "wife," as the Philistine woman is now called, is given by her father to another man. It is at this time that Samson's fox-escapade destroys the fields of the Philistines, who retaliate by burning at the stake Samson's wife and her father. Samson takes revenge, first by slaughtering many of the Philistines. When the Philistines attack the men of Judah, however, he allows the latter to bind him and deliver him to the Philistines. Then he breaks his bonds, seizes the jawbone of an ass, and with it kills a thousand Philistines. Thereafter, he judges Israel in peace for twenty years.

A subsequent adventure takes place in Gaza, where Samson has fallen in love with Delilah, another Philistine woman. Bribed by her fellow countrymen to find the secret of Samson's great strength, Delilah uses her feminine wiles on the Hebrew hero. Thrice he gives her false answers, and thrice he breaks the bonds she puts on him. Then he foolishly tells her the truth—that the secret of his might lies in his unshaven hair. As soon as he falls asleep, the treacherous Delilah shaves his head and calls the Philistines, who put out Samson's eyes, bind him in fetters, and throw him into prison. Later, when his hair has grown long again, the Philistines add to the degradation of the fallen hero by forcing him to play the fool. They require him to amuse a great crowd gathered for a festival in honor of their god Dagon. When he is led into the temple, Samson prays to the Lord for strength so that he may avenge himself. God answers his prayer:

Samson leans with all his might upon the middle pillars support-
ing the temple, and pushes them down, so that the temple falls
and kills three thousand Philistines as well as Samson himself.
Samson's brothers recover the body of the hero and bury it.

Post-Exilic Appendixes to the Book (Chs. 17–21). At the end
of the book of Judges are added two narratives which are un-
related to the exploits of the judges but which tell about the
same period in history.[7]

MIGRATION OF THE DANITES (Chs. 17–18). This is an account
of how the tribe of Dan (which up to this time has found no
place in which to settle) conquers the Sidonian city of Laish,
renames it "Dan," and then makes an ephod * to be worshiped.
Perhaps the strangest thing about the tale is that the author nowhere condemns the Danites for idol-worship, but is content to
remark: "In those days there was no king in Israel, but every
man did that which was right in his own eyes."

THE OFFENSE OF GIBEAH (Chs. 19–21). This is a brutal story
of revenge. The concubine of a certain Levite of Mount Ephraim
is raped to death by a group of Benjamites in the city of Gibeah.
The Levite cuts the body of the dead woman into twelve pieces
and sends each one to a different part of Canaan in order to
shock the various tribes into helping him seek vengeance. The
Israelites of other tribes gather "together as one man"—perhaps
an indication of increasing national unity.[8] First they ask that
the offending group from Gibeah be put to death. When this is
refused, they wage war against the Benjamites and kill all but
six hundred whom they later provide with wives from Jabesh-
gilead and Shiloh.

I AND II SAMUEL AND I KINGS 1–2: GROWTH OF
MONARCHY TEMPERED BY THEOCRACY

The four books which in the English Bible are called I and II
Samuel and I and II Kings were once a single continuous narrative. The Hebrew text, lacking vowels, required the use of only

* The word *ephod* is apparently used to denote two different articles at
different times. Sometimes (as in Ex. 28:6-12) it is a garment, especially
one worn by a priest; at other times it is a box, an ark, or a tentlike structure, used as an instrument of divination. For a discussion of the problem,
see George B. Caird, introduction to I and II Samuel, *The Interpreter's
Bible,* II, 872-874.

two scrolls; in the Jewish Scriptures these were known, respectively, as the book of Samuel and the book of Kings. The Greek text (the Septuagint) filled four scrolls; the artificial division into four parts has been continued in English versions. Our name for the first two books is misleading, for only eight of the forty-five chapters are primarily concerned with Samuel; he dies before any of the events in II Samuel take place. The first two chapters of I Kings belong logically with the "David cycle" found in the books of Samuel.

I and II Samuel are drawn principally from two sources: [9] (a) The "early" source was probably written about the middle of the tenth century B.C. There is little doubt that the author of this document was a priest, a contemporary of David, and an eyewitness of many of the events which he records. Many commentators are convinced that this author was Abiathar, the priest and close friend of David who was discarded by Solomon (see I Kings 2:26). A modern Biblical scholar, Alice Parmelee, claims that he, not Herodotus, deserves the title "the father of history":

As far as we know, this volume, written by a Hebrew priest around 1000 B.C., is the oldest book of history in the world. With no models to follow, Abiathar, or whoever the author was, created the art of history writing.[10]

(b) The "late" source is of uncertain date; some parts seem to have been written early (c. 900 B.C.), and others much later, perhaps as late as 700 B.C. The authors' names and identities are unknown. According to some Biblical scholars, it was probably during the seventh century B.C. that these two sources were conflated with many discrepancies, repetitions, and contradictions. About 550 B.C. some reviser, following the Deuteronomic traditions, re-edited the whole narrative. This was the last major revision of the books, but there were several significant later interpolations, some believed to be as late as the fifth century B.C.[11]

The two books of Samuel, plus the opening two chapters of I Kings, depict the transition of the Hebrew nation from a loose confederation of tribes under the semi-theocratic government of the judges into a unified monarchy. This transition extended over slightly more than half a century (c. 1030—c. 973 B.C.). Another important development during the period was the rise of prophets, lay leaders who in later centuries were destined to figure prominently in the religious and political affairs of the Jewish people.

Samuel is perhaps the finest narrative book in the Bible. The style of the book is simple; the narrative, easy, unified, and progressive, incident following incident as in a well-connected story. The details are always sufficient to make the pictures and incidents vivid, distinct, and realistic, yet they are never dry or cumbersome. But the chief glory of the book is its masterly characterization. Here are real men and women, heroic enough to have a godlike vision of truth and righteous behavior, yet they are true citizens of the earth where there is nothing absolutely perfect.[12]

The books of Samuel consist principally of the biographies of Samuel himself, of Saul, and of David. These stories overlap each other, for each of the three main characters becomes involved in the lives of the other two. In order to present three unified cycles, some reorganization of Biblical material is necessary.

Samuel the Kingmaker [13] (I Sam. 1—8 and 9—25, *passim*). Like the judges of earlier generations, Samuel appears at a time of national emergency. The last of the judges and one of the first of the prophets, he is at the same time a priest, a soothsayer, a spokesman for God, and a political leader. In the two latter roles he is a prototype of such great prophets as Elijah and Isaiah.

BIRTH AND CHILDHOOD (I Sam. 1–3). The story opens with an account of the quasi-miraculous conception of Samuel by Hannah.* This unhappy woman, one of the two wives of Elkanah, cries to the Lord "in bitterness of soul" because she is barren, and she promises the Lord that if he will give her a son, she will dedicate him to God "all the days of his life." Eli, the priest of the temple at Shiloh, who has watched her weeping and praying silently, accuses her of drunkenness; she, of course, denies the charge. The Lord grants her petition, and in due time Hannah triumphantly presents the baby Samuel to Eli. Then follows Hannah's famous song of praise (I Sam. 2:1-10).†

Hannah leaves Samuel with Eli in the temple at Shiloh; there the old priest brings him up in the service of the Lord. The historian gives an appealing picture of Hannah's coming once a year to offer a sacrifice and to bring a little coat for her son.

---

* See note, p. 51.

† Comparable to Mary's Magnificat (Luke 1:46-55).

When Eli has grown very old, he is saddened by the fact that his two sons, apparently in succession for the judgeship, have fallen into evil ways. In contrast with these sons, Samuel has continued to grow "in favour both with the Lord, and also with men." One day Samuel receives a special summons from the Lord. While sleeping, the young boy hears a voice calling his name. Thinking it to be Eli's, he runs to the priest; but Eli denies having called him and tells him to go back to sleep. The call comes again, and again Eli tells Samuel to return to his bed. When the voice calls the third time, the priest tells the lad that it is God who is calling and that the next time he must answer: "Speak, Lord; for thy servant heareth." A fourth time God calls, and now he foretells to Samuel the destruction of the sons of Eli for their iniquity. Samuel soon afterward is recognized as a seer and a prophet of the Lord.

ADMINISTRATION (I Sam. 4—8). When the Philistines wage a victorious battle against the Israelites, thousands of the men of Israel (including the two sons of Eli) are slain, and the Ark of the Covenant is captured. On hearing of the disaster, Eli, now ninety-eight years old, falls dead. Samuel succeeds him as judge of Israel.

The capture of the Ark, though a major disaster to Israel, brings misfortune to the Philistines. First, they set the Ark in the temple of their god Dagon, but on the following morning the statue of Dagon is found fallen and broken. The Ark is moved from Ashdod to Gath and then to Ekron, and the inhabitants of these cities are smitten with a plague of emerods (tumors). In terror the Philistines abandon the Ark in Bethshemesh, and it is reclaimed by the Israelites, who repent their sins and completely subdue the enemy. Samuel thereafter judges Israel— apparently in peace and prosperity—for many years.

When he has grown old, he turns the government over to his sons Joel and Abiah. But these sons are corrupt, and they so "pervert judgment" that the elders of Israel clamor for a monarch: "Make us a king to judge us like all the nations." Samuel feels that the people have rejected God as their king. He prays to the Lord but is instructed to give in to the popular demand and to find a king of Israel; he is to warn the people, however, of the evils of kingship. (The warning which Samuel accordingly delivers [I Sam. 8:11-18] is probably a reflection of the opinions of the Biblical historian, writing in retrospect.)

RETIREMENT AND FURTHER PROPHETIC ACTIVITIES (I Sam. 9–25, *passim*). The remainder of Samuel's deeds belong more properly to the cycles of tales about Saul and David and therefore require only the briefest mention here. The old prophet anoints Saul to be king of Israel, but later on, reconsidering matters, turns against him and anoints David (instead of any of Saul's sons) as future successor to the throne. Thus, despite the establishment of a monarchy, Samuel continues to exercise a powerful influence on the political affairs of Israel all the days of his life. He dies during the reign of Saul (I Sam. 25:1).

The Tragedy of Saul[14] (I Sam. 9–31, *passim*). The sad story of the first king of Israel is, as Mary Ellen Chase points out, like a Greek tragedy. On the whole a good man, Saul has a "tragic flaw," which, along with outside circumstances, brings about his downfall.

The son of a prosperous farmer of the tribe of Benjamin, he is described as "a choice young man, and a goodly . . . from his shoulders and upward he was higher than any of the people" * (I Sam. 9:2). He evidently has a forceful and attractive personality, for he succeeds in uniting the people and in maintaining their loyalty throughout his reign. But he is subject to fits of melancholia. He is the prey of his "complex and passionate nature" which holds "within itself the seeds of despondency and madness." [15]

Israel's debt to Saul is considerable, for in addition to unifying the tribes, he wins important victories over nearly all the nation's enemies, including the Philistines, and he establishes a base on the east bank of the Jordan.

ANOINTING AND EARLY VICTORIES (I Sam. 9:1–10:27, 11:1-15, and 14:47-52). On a mission to find his father's lost asses, Saul seeks the advice of the seer Samuel ("he that is now called a Prophet was before time called a Seer"). The Lord tells Samuel that this tall and handsome youth is the one chosen to become king. Samuel anoints Saul with oil and announces to him God's

---

* Extraordinary stature is a characteristic of the traditional "tragic hero." One should compare the various descriptions of Tamerlane and also the ancient Greek custom of increasing the height of tragic heroes by the use of the cothurnus (thick-soled shoe).

will that he be the ruler of Israel. Saul is overwhelmed and later hides when Samuel tries to present him to a throng of people summoned to convene at Mizpah. The convention chooses him by lot, however, and all the people shout: "God save the king!"

The new king's first official act is to defeat the Ammonites who are besieging Jabesh-gilead. Subsequently he leads his army victoriously against the Moabites, the Ammonites, the Edomites, the kings of Zobah, and the Amalekites. He repulses the Philistines, too, but is unable to put an end to their raids on his land.

SHORTCOMINGS AND REJECTION (I Sam. 10:8, 13:8-14, and 15:1-35). Modern commentators are inclined to regard the Philistines' slaying of Saul and his sons and David's accession to the throne of Israel as historical events which require no explanation. The Deuteronomic historian, however, evidently feels that Saul's failure to found a dynasty does need to be accounted for, especially since God directed Samuel to anoint Saul, thereby enabling him to become the potential progenitor of a dynasty.[16] The historian's usual explanation of a calamity is that it is a punishment inflicted by God for wrongdoing. So Saul is charged with being guilty of two things: usurpation of priestly functions and failure to obey divine commands. Therefore Samuel, acting as God's agent, rejects Saul twice.

The first rejection precedes a great battle against the Philistines. An important item in the preparations for the conflict is the offering of a sacrifice to God. The aged Samuel promises to be present to officiate, but fails to appear at the appointed time. Saul himself presides at the offering. On arrival, Samuel denounces Saul for usurping the priestly duties; he proclaims that the kingdom shall be taken away from Saul and given to another. In spite of the rebuke, Saul and his son Jonathan win a great victory over the Philistines.

Now Samuel sends Saul to destroy the Amalekites. He instructs the king to kill every living thing—"man and woman, infant and suckling, ox and sheep, camel and ass." Again Saul is victorious, but his soldiers bring back alive some sheep and oxen to sacrifice to the Lord, and Saul spares the life of Agag, the captive king of Amalek. In great wrath once more, Samuel asks: "Hath the Lord as great delight in burnt offerings and sacrifices, as in obeying the voice of the Lord? Behold, to obey is better than sacrifice, and to hearken than the fat of rams."

For the second time, Samuel announces that the Lord has rejected Saul as king of Israel. In deep sorrow and repentance, Saul humbly promises to obey the Lord and to worship him. Samuel then hacks Agag to pieces with a sword.

DECLINE (I Sam. 16:14-23 and 18–27, *passim*). Having rejected Saul, Samuel anoints David to be the successor to the throne. As the spirit of the Lord descends upon David, it departs from Saul, and "an evil spirit from the Lord" troubles him. Renounced by Samuel and even by God, well might Saul be depressed. He calls for a musician to play for him and relieve his melancholy. Ironically (or perhaps providentially), it is David who is summoned. Immediately Saul learns to love him and soon makes him his armor-bearer. Thereafter whenever the fit of melancholy falls, David plays on the harp, and the evil spirit leaves Saul.

According to another story,* Saul's melancholia is principally the result of his jealousy over David's success as a soldier. To reward David for killing the giant Goliath and for defeating the Philistines, Saul makes him a high officer in the army. But when the women sing: "Saul hath slain his thousands, and David his ten thousands," Saul's jealousy knows no bounds. Twice he hurls a javelin at David, who each time eludes the weapon. Again Saul sends messengers to kill David in his sleep, but Michal (Saul's own daughter, who has been given to David in marriage) enables her husband to escape.

In the meantime, David has formed a close friendship with Jonathan, Saul's son, who tries to convince his father that David has done no wrong; but Saul will not listen, and David has to flee for his life. He finds refuge at one place and then another; Saul pursues him wherever he goes. David has an opportunity to kill Saul, but only cuts off a piece of the sleeping king's robe and later shows it to him from a distance. Saul is overwhelmed with remorse: "Is this thy voice, my son David?" He weeps and says to David: "Thou art more righteous than I: for thou hast rewarded me good, whereas I have rewarded thee evil." Unfortunately the remorse is short-lived, and the pursuit recommences. Again David has a chance to kill Saul, but declines to raise his hand against the Lord's anointed. At length David escapes to

---

* Obviously from a different source, for in this second account, David is introduced as an unknown; see I Sam. 17:55-58.

the land of the Philistines, where he is befriended by the king of Gath.

DEATH (I Sam. 28 and 31 and II Sam. 1:1-16). Saul feels that his son Jonathan and his daughter Michal have turned against him; he knows that his former friend David has joined the enemy Philistines, and he suffers because the Lord has forsaken him (Samuel, incidentally, has died during the course of Saul's pursuit of David). Saul presents a pitiable figure as he surveys the multitudes of Philistines arrayed against him at Gilboa. He is afraid and his heart trembles. He seeks the aid of the Lord, but the Lord does not answer him. There is bitter irony in Saul's next move. He has formerly banished all soothsayers and sorcerers from his kingdom, but now he seeks the aid of one of those he has banished. He employs the witch of Endor to call up the spirit of Samuel. That spirit asks: "Why hast thou disquieted me, to bring me up?" Saul answers: "I am sore distressed; for the Philistines make war against me, and God is departed from me, and answereth me no more, neither by prophets, nor by dreams; therefore I have called thee, that thou mayest make known unto me what I shall do." The spirit holds out no hope: the Philistines will win the battle, Saul and his sons will be killed, and David will take over the kingdom.

In a spirit of desperation comparable to that of Macbeth meeting the hosts of Macduff at Dunsinane, Saul joins in the battle against the Philistines. The tale is briefly told by the historian. The men of Israel flee from the enemy. Many of the Israelites are slain, including Saul's sons Jonathan, Abinadab, and Melchishua. Saul himself falls upon his own sword; his body is captured by the enemy, but is later retrieved by the Israelites, burned, and the bones buried at Jabesh.

A different account of Saul's death (apparently intended by the Biblical historian to be understood as a mere story) is given in the first chapter of II Samuel. Here an Amalekite comes to David and says that he himself slew Saul at Saul's request. David has the Amalekite killed for slaying the Lord's anointed.

David, Founder of the Royal Line (I Sam. 16–30, *passim* and II Sam.–I Kings 2). David was incomparably the greatest of the Hebrew kings. An able military leader and an astute administrator of public affairs, he extended the boundaries of the country to their greatest limit (including areas in Transjordan to the east and to Tyre in the north), inspired the fear and respect of foreign neighbors, established the national capital at Jerusalem, filled the coffers of the royal treasury, and founded a dynasty which was to rule for more than four hundred years. It is not surprising that the reign of David is traditionally regarded as the most glorious era in Jewish history or that it was the Davidic line from which, during centuries of oppression, the Hebrews expected a Messiah.

The Biblical historian devotes about half of I Samuel and virtually all of II Samuel to the stories of David's public achievements and private affairs.

ANOINTMENT AND RISE TO FAME (I Sam. 16:1–18:16). After rejecting Saul, the Lord directs Samuel to go to Bethlehem and there to anoint one of the sons of Jesse (which of the sons God does not designate) as future king. The historian gives an exciting account: Samuel says that he fears to go lest Saul kill him; the Lord tells him to pretend that he is going merely to offer a sacrifice. The elders of Bethlehem tremble at Samuel's unexpected appearance in their town, and they ask him: "Comest thou peaceably?" He assures them that his mission is peaceful and invites them to a sacrifice. He sends a special invitation to Jesse and his sons. The people sense the significance of the situation, and as the eldest of Jesse's sons comes forth, they whisper: "Surely the Lord's anointed is before him." One by one, seven stalwart sons are presented to the old seer. When Samuel asks whether these are all of Jesse's children, Jesse answers that only the youngest remains and that he is keeping the sheep. Samuel says, "Send and fetch him." This one is David, and when he appears—"ruddy, and withal of a beautiful countenance, and goodly to look to"—the Lord says, "Arise, anoint him: for this is he." Samuel anoints him, and thenceforth the spirit of the Lord dwells upon David.

The next appearance of David (I Sam. 16:14-23, discussed above) is as Saul's musician and armor-bearer.

The historian now evidently draws upon another source of information, for a conflicting story is told of David's introduction to the court of Saul. The Israelites are once again at war with the Philistines, who are led by Goliath, a mighty champion nearly ten feet high. This giant mocks the people of Israel and challenges them to produce somebody suitable to meet him in single combat. David (who is now described as keeper of his father's sheep) is sent on an errand to deliver food to his brothers in Saul's army. Hearing of Goliath's insults to God's people, David offers to fight the giant. Saul calls for David and equips him with armor, but David finds it too heavy, lays it aside, and goes into combat armed only with a slingshot and five pebbles. Goliath is outraged that such a stripling should be sent against him, and he curses David by his pagan gods. David replies: "I come to thee in the name of the Lord of hosts, the God of the armies of Israel, whom thou has defied." Then he slings a stone, which sinks into his opponent's forehead. David cuts off Goliath's head with the giant's own sword.* The Philistines flee, and the Israelites pursue them and gain a great victory.

This is the point where David launches his career as a popular hero and so begins to arouse Saul's jealousy.

DAVID AND JONATHAN (I Sam. 18:1-4, 19:1-7, 20:1-42, 23:16-18; II Sam. 1:17-27, 4:4, and 9:1-13). In the meantime, David has formed a close friendship with Saul's son Jonathan. The historian says that Jonathan's soul is "knit with the soul of David" and that Jonathan loves him "as his own soul." Jonathan gives David his robe and other garments, "even to his sword, and to his bow, and to his girdle." When Saul tries to kill David, Jonathan warns his friend to hide and then attempts to convince Saul that David is innocent of any offense. He espouses David's cause with such warmth that Saul is provoked to anger. Saul calls Jonathan the "son of a perverse rebellious woman" and tries vainly to kill him with a javelin. Jonathan hastens to David's hiding place and advises him to flee. After they have bidden each other a tearful farewell, David departs into exile. Only once more do they see each other, and then for just a short time while David is hiding in the wilderness.

The deaths of Jonathan and Saul inspire one of the finest

---

* These stories of the youthful David show several folk elements: (1) the parade of the seven elder sons first and the presentation of the youngest only upon request; (2) discrepancy in the traditions about the killing of Goliath (in II Sam. 21:19 his slaying is attributed to one Elhanan); (3) the use of a special sword for beheading a monster; compare Beowulf's decapitation of the corpse of Grendel; and (4) the offer of riches and a king's daughter (Merab, I Sam. 17:25) to whoever will overcome a monster. The lack of any further reference to David's use of a slingshot in warfare is noteworthy.

poems in the Bible—the only one except for a brief elegy over Abner (according to the noted Biblical scholar Mary Ellen Chase [17]) that may be attributed unquestionably to David. It is a dirge laden with deep personal sorrow:

> The beauty of Israel is slain upon thy high places.
> How are the mighty fallen! . . .
> Saul and Jonathan were lovely and pleasant in their lives,
> And in their death they were not divided.
> They were swifter than eagles,
> They were stronger than lions. . . .
> How are the mighty fallen in the midst of the battle!
> O Jonathan, thou wast slain in thine high places.
> I am distressed for thee, my brother Jonathan:
> Very pleasant hast thou been unto me:
> Thy love to me was wonderful,
> Passing the love of woman. (II Sam. 1:19-26)

A sequel to this story reveals the enduring quality of David's affection for Jonathan. After David has become well established as king of Israel, Mephibosheth, the lame * son of Jonathan, is brought before him. Now, it was customary for an Oriental ruler to wipe out all the descendants of a former ruler in order to prevent their attempting to gain the throne for themselves (compare Abimelech's slaughter of his half-brothers, related in Judges 9:5). David does the unexpected: when he discovers the identity of Mephibosheth, instead of killing him, he graciously takes him into the king's household, so that Mephibosheth thereafter eats at David's own table.

PUBLIC ACHIEVEMENTS (II Sam. 2—8 and 10). Soon after Saul is killed in battle, God directs David to return to his native land. A delegation from the tribe of Judah meets him and proclaims him king; he sets up his capital at Hebron. The other tribes, however, adhere to Ishbosheth, one of Saul's sons. Civil war follows, Ishbosheth is slain, and David is accepted by all the tribes as their king (II Sam. 5:1).

One of his first acts as king of a united Israel is to conquer the fortified city of Jerusalem (or Zion), held by the Jebusites; this he makes his new capital (II Sam. 5:6-9). He brings here the

---

* Mephibosheth is lame because his nurse dropped him when he was five years old. The implication is that David adopts him not out of pity for his lameness but out of affection for Jonathan.

Ark of the Covenant and plans to build a temple for the Ark to stay in, but is told by the Lord that the task will be accomplished by David's son. God promises, however, to make David's royal lineage and his kingdom prosper forever.

In the court at Jerusalem are several interesting people who are to play significant roles in the drama of David's public and domestic life: Joab, the commander of the army—treacherous, ruthless, and vengeful; Nathan, a bold and upright prophet, who fears the Lord more than he does David; and Abiathar, a learned and observant priest (and possibly the royal historian).

Surrounded by these and many other devoted followers, David begins a reign which, though destined to be long and glorious, is marred by foreign wars and internal rebellions. At different times David defeats the Moabites, the Syrians, the Edomites, and the Ammonites.

DAVID AND MICHAL (I Sam. 18:17-27, 19:11-17, 25:44; II Sam. 3:13-16, 6:16-23). David has many wives and many children, and some of these bring him great sorrow. One of the most pathetic domestic stories is concerned with Michal, his first wife. Soon after Saul has grown jealous of David's popularity, Saul learns that his own daughter Michal loves David. Perceiving a way in which he may be able to destroy his rival, Saul agrees to the match provided that David will give him as a "marriage gift" * a hundred foreskins of the Philistines. David accepts the proposal, kills not one hundred but two hundred Philistines, presents their foreskins to Saul, and marries Michal. In his jealous hatred, Saul sends some henchmen to kill David, apparently before the marriage is consummated.[18] Michal learns of the approach of the assassins, deceives them by placing a dummy in David's bed, and enables David to escape by letting him down through a window. While David is in exile, Saul gives Michal to Phalti (or Phaltiel or Paltiel), to whom she transfers her love and with whom she lives for several years. During this period David acquires several wives and concubines. When he becomes king, he takes Michal away from Phalti, who is heartbroken over having to give her up: he goes "with her along weeping behind her. . . ." Michal is later said to despise David

---

* In ancient Hebrew society it was customary for the groom to present a gift to the bride's father. See Caird, exegesis, *The Interpreter's Bible*, II, 984.

"in her heart" when she sees him, clad only in a priest's apron, "leaping and dancing" to celebrate the coming of the Ark to Jerusalem. She greets him with the sarcastic gibe: "How glorious was the king of Israel today, who uncovered himself today in the eyes of the handmaids of his servants, as one of the vain fellows shamelessly uncovereth himself!" David punishes her by refusing thenceforth to cohabit with her. Thus the matter ends unhappily for all involved.

DAVID AND BATHSHEBA (II Sam. 11–12). David is guilty of a most reprehensible act as the result of his passion for a woman:

One year during the season "when kings go forth to battle," * David himself stays in Jerusalem but sends his army, under Joab, to fight the Ammonites. While on the roof of his palace, he looks down into a neighboring courtyard and sees a woman bathing, and the woman is "very beautiful to look upon." He ascertains that she is Bathsheba, the wife of Uriah the Hittite. Ignoring the fact that she belongs to another man, David has her brought to his palace and makes her his mistress. When she later reveals to him that she is going to bear a child, he gives orders that Uriah be put into the "hottest" part of the battlefront and that the other soldiers "retire" from him, "that he may be smitten, and die." All happens as David has planned: Uriah is killed, and David marries Bathsheba.

Retribution follows this act of injustice. Believing that the Lord is not only the God of the Covenant and the Hebrew God of battle but also a Deity interested in righteous behavior, the historian tells us that David's deed has so displeased the Lord that the Lord sends the prophet Nathan to rebuke David. Nathan tells David a story about a rich man and a poor man. The former had "exceeding many flocks and herds," but "the poor man had nothing, save one little ewe lamb, which he had bought and nourished up: and it grew up together with him, and with his children; it did eat of his own meat, and drank of his own cup, and lay in his bosom, and was unto him as a daughter." When entertaining a traveler, the rich man spared his own flock, killed the poor man's ewe lamb, and served it. On hearing this tale of injustice, David is angry and vows to have the rich man restore the

---

* Biblical scholars are in disagreement as to whether ancient Oriental kings "went to battle" in the springtime when the weather was propitious, or whether they went in the fall when all crops had been harvested.

lamb fourfold. Then comes the most dramatic part of the story. Nathan unflinchingly says: "Thou art the man." He goes on to tell David that God is displeased over the murder of Uriah and the seizure of Bathsheba. David is humbly penitent: "I have sinned against the Lord." The Lord forgives him but punishes him by causing Bathsheba's son to die. Soon, however, Bathsheba conceives again and bears another son, Solomon.

DAVID AND ABSALOM (II Sam. 13—19). Some of David's other children bring great sorrow to their father. Amnon conceives a violent passion for his half-sister Tamar, a virgin. He pretends illness and asks that Tamar bring food to him. As soon as he and she are alone, he ravishes her. When Absalom, Tamar's full brother, hears of the outrage, he plots vengeance against Amnon. For two years he awaits a favorable opportunity. At last he invites all of David's sons to a sheepshearing. Amnon attends, and when he is "merry with wine," Absalom's servants kill him. Absalom himself flees into Syria. David is grief-stricken over the death of Amnon, but apparently mourns even more over the absence of his son Absalom (13:38-39).

After Absalom has remained in exile three years, David sends Joab to bring him back to Jerusalem; but David refuses to see his son for two more years. Absalom summons Joab to come to him, hoping that he can persuade the trusted general to intercede for him; but Joab will not come. Absalom spitefully sets fire to Joab's barley field. At length Joab does persuade David to see Absalom, and apparently father and son are reconciled.

Absalom, however, is bitter and disaffected, ambitious and revengeful. Knowing that neither primogeniture nor hereditary succession to the kingship has been established in the new kingdom, he decides to employ his own methods for usurping the throne. He acquires "chariots and horses, and fifty men to run before him" (the ancient equivalent of Hitler's "storm troopers"), makes rash promises to every malcontent, disparages his father's abilities, and soon steals "the hearts of the men of Israel" (15:6). When he feels that he has a sufficiently large following, he goes to Hebron (under the pretext of fulfilling a religious vow), and from this former capital of Judah he sends out messengers all over the country to announce: "Absalom reigneth in Hebron." The conspiracy thrives. Many men, including Ahithophel, one of David's trusted counselors, join Absalom.

Fearing military disaster and perhaps seeking a more strategic military position,[19] David flees from Jerusalem, taking with him his family, the priests Zadok and Abiathar, the Levites, and the Ark of the Covenant. Then he decides to have Zadok and Abiathar carry the Ark back to the city; these two and Hushai, another faithful supporter, are to remain in Jerusalem as his spies and informants. Absalom triumphantly moves into the capital.

David's band continues its flight and crosses the Jordan into the land of Gilead. Ahithophel advises Absalom to let him pursue David with twelve thousand men. Hushai, pretending to be a deserter from David's camp, disagrees with Ahithophel and advises Absalom to gather a great host from all over Israel and to lead the host himself. When Absalom follows the advice of Hushai, Ahithophel hangs himself.

Befriended by some of the Gileadites and Ammonites, David makes a stand at the wood of Ephraim and prepares to fight against the rebel army. Before the battle he warns his men not to harm his traitorous son: "Deal gently for my sake with the young man, even with Absalom." The fighting now begins, and the rebels are ignominiously defeated. In the course of the battle Absalom himself is riding on a mule. As he passes under an oak, his head is caught in a fork of the tree, the mule runs from under him, and he is left hanging helpless. When the news of this event reaches Joab, he hurries to the spot, and, in spite of David's injunction to spare the young man, hurls three darts into Absalom's heart. Then he buries the body in a pit.

When David hears of his son's death, his grief is crushing. The lament that he utters is one of the most heart-rending cries in all literature: "O my son Absalom, my son, my son Absalom! would God I had died for thee, O Absalom, my son, my son!"

Soon thereafter David and all his band return to Jerusalem. Joab is apparently forgiven for disobedience and allowed to remain in an influential position. David pardons many of those who refused to follow him—including the lame Mephibosheth; and he rewards the Gileadites and others who have supported him. The rebellion is at an end.

DAVID'S DECLINING YEARS AND DEATH (II Sam. 20–24; I Kings 1–2). As David approaches old age, there are several occurrences which prevent his reign from being tranquil: a revolt of the northern tribes (II Sam. 20), a three-year famine (II Sam.

21:1-14), a three-year plague (II Sam. 24), and four more battles against the Philistines (II Sam. 22—23). A census at this time records 1,300,000 men of military age—a dubious population figure (II Sam. 24:1-9).

In the account of one of the battles against the Philistines, the historian records an incident which adds to the attractiveness of David's character. The aging king voices a longing for some of the water from the well beside the gate of Bethlehem, now held by the Philistines. At the risk of their lives David's three mightiest men break through the enemy lines, procure some of the water, and bring it back to David. Deeply touched, David will not drink, but pours the water out, saying, "Be it far from me, O Lord, that I should do this: is not this the blood of the men that went in jeopardy of their lives?"

When David reaches extreme old age, he is adjudged by political and religious experts to be senile and unfit to rule. He is willing to abdicate (I Kings 1:48), but when the choice of a successor must be made, his advisers split into two factions. One faction (including Joab and Abiathar) supports Adonijah, the eldest surviving son; succession by primogeniture, however, has not yet been established as a custom in Israel. The other faction supports Bathsheba's son Solomon. When Bathsheba hears that Adonijah has attracted a large following and has had himself proclaimed king, she and Nathan go to David and remind him of an old promise [20] to make Solomon his successor. David orders Nathan to anoint Solomon, messengers to blow trumpets, and the people to shout: "God save king Solomon!" When Adonijah hears the uproar, he flees to the Temple and begs Solomon's mercy. Temporarily Solomon allows him to depart in peace.

David charges his son Solomon to obey God's commandments. After a reign of "forty" years, David dies and is buried in Jerusalem.

Adonijah pleads with Bathsheba until she agrees to request Solomon to give him Abishag as his wife (Abishag is a young woman who has been appointed to sleep with David and so keep him warm in his old age). Solomon construes the request as a sign of royal pretensions on Adonijah's part (inasmuch as it was an ancient Semitic custom for a new king to take over his predecessor's women),[21] and he has Adonijah executed. He also orders the banishment of Abiathar; and, obeying an injunction formerly laid upon him by David, he decrees the execution of Joab (who is guilty of the murder of two military leaders under David's protection).

Thus Solomon establishes his kingdom.

I KINGS 3–22 AND II KINGS: TRIUMPH AND DOWNFALL OF MONARCHY TEMPERED BY THEOCRACY

Like the two books of Samuel, I and II Kings originally formed one continuous Hebrew scroll, and the division into "books" was made in the Septuagint. The books derive their name from the fact that they deal with the reigns of the kings of Israel and Judah from the days of David to the Exile.

The writing and revising of I and II Kings was a long process, perhaps extending over nearly eight centuries.[22] The principal steps seem to have been as follows:

A short while before the death of King Josiah of Judah (609 B.C.), some writer whose name is unknown composed the major portion of I and II Kings (I Kings 2:1-12, 3–22 and II Kings 1:1–23:25a). He drew on the following no-longer-extant sources: (1) the Acts of Solomon (mentioned in I Kings 11:41), probably written in the tenth century B.C.; (2) the Book of the Chronicles of the Kings of Israel (mentioned in I Kings 14:19 and in sixteen other places), finished about 725 B.C.; (3) the Book of the Chronicles of the Kings of Judah (mentioned in I Kings 14:29 and in fourteen other places), finished about 590 B.C.; and (4) tales of the Southern Kingdom, by the prophet Isaiah, written about 715-700 B.C.

At some time between 610 and 538 B.C. two successive editors of strong Deuteronomic tendencies revised the manuscript, adding the conclusion (II Kings 23:25b–25:30) and interpolating many passages of northern origin, especially those relating to Ahab, Elijah, and Elisha.

There is evidence that various post-Exilic editors continued to revise the books of Kings—perhaps as late as the middle of the second century B.C. At some unknown date the passages which now form I Kings 1 and 2 were severed from the manuscript of II Samuel and made to serve as an introduction to the reign of Solomon.

The purpose of the original compiler (probably in 610 B.C.) was to prove the necessity of obeying the Deuteronomic law. He illustrated this principle by demonstrating how "good" kings (that is, those who fulfilled the law), like Josiah, were successful and prosperous, whereas the "wicked" ones, like Ahab, brought disaster upon themselves and their country. Thus the narrative in the two books of Kings is not a history in the sense of a full and careful record of the important events that took place in Palestine during the period covered. "Rather it is an attempt to present in systematic order the development of certain attitudes toward race and religious ideals that finally led to the great disaster [the Babylonian captivity]." [23]

The author's method is clear and consistent. First he tells of the reign of Solomon. Then, after the division of the country into the kingdoms of Israel and Judah, he tries to deal contemporaneously with the events of both kingdoms; that is, he begins with the accession of one king, tells about the events in his reign, and then goes on to the history of the other kingdom during the same period. For each king of Judah he gives the date of accession (in "terms of the year of the reigning king of Israel" [24]), the age of the king at the time of his accession, the name of the queen mother, and a summary of the king's attitude toward the Deuteronomic law. For each king of Israel he gives the date of accession (in terms of the year of the reigning king of Judah), the name of his capital, the length of his reign, and his opinion of the king's ethical and religious nature. This framework is readily adaptable to the author's didactic purpose.

Although I and II Kings make up "a religious philosophy of history rather than a history proper, yet as always with the Jewish writers the ideas are conveyed through such vivid pictures of concrete personalities that the latter have for us a value in themselves over and above the principles they are designed to illustrate." [25]

The two books of Kings exhibit the Jewish nation at its peak of fame and prosperity under Solomon, its division into two kingdoms, its moral and spiritual decay (a decay arrested from time to time by the efforts of prophets and "good" kings), its growing fear of invasion by Assyria and Babylonia, and, finally, its complete subjugation by those foreign powers. During this period of about four centuries, the role of the prophets—those lay spokesmen for God—increased in importance, so that sometimes they wielded great political influence and vied with the official ecclesiastical groups for the religious and ethical leadership of the people. At all times, religion, not mere political organization, united the Hebrew people, even when they were physically divided into separate kingdoms. The laws, rights, and duties of the kings were set forth as only one portion, not the main portion, of the religious tradition.

The "Golden Age" of Solomon (I Kings 3—11). In the description by the Biblical historian, the reign of Solomon (c. 960-c. 922 B.C.) was the "Golden Age" of Israel—an era of peace and prosperity, when the people were "eating and drinking, and making merry" (I Kings 4:20) and when they "dwelt safely, every man under his vine and under his fig tree" (I Kings 4:25). The boundaries of the kingdom stretched from the Euphrates to the land of the Philistines and on to the borders of Egypt (I Kings 4:21). Modern historians, however, suspect that the era was one of false prosperity, that Solomon's lavish expenditures brought the nation to the verge of bankruptcy, and that his conscription of labor and the levying of high taxes (as well as his later tolerance of foreign gods) caused much popular unrest, ending in the division of the kingdom at Solomon's death. They point out that, except in the capital, most of the kingdom did not enjoy great prosperity most of the time. Towns at a distance from Jerusalem had a poor, peasant economy (in contrast to Solomon's wealth and imported luxuries) without extremes of utter poverty and great riches. Prior to the eighth century, debtors and the poor had to be protected, reducing somewhat the disparity between rich and poor. On the other hand, defaulting debtors might have to become slaves. (But religious tradition made it a capital crime to kidnap an Israelite in order to sell him into slavery.)

SOLOMON'S WISDOM AND RICHES (I Kings 3—4 and 9:10—10:29). According to the Biblical author, the greatest glories of the epoch are the splendor of the court and the wisdom of the sovereign: "King Solomon exceeded all the kings of the earth for riches and for wisdom" (I Kings 10:23). His wisdom is a special gift of God. Soon after Solomon ascends the throne, the Lord appears to him in a dream and asks what gift he would like to have. Already wise, Solomon answers, "Give therefore thy servant an understanding heart to judge thy people, that I may discern between good and bad; for who is able to judge this thy so great a people?" Because he has requested wisdom rather than long life or wealth, God promises to give him not only wisdom but also riches and honor.

The first manifestation of Solomon's great probity is his famous decision concerning the disputed child: each of two harlots claims to be the mother of a little boy. When Solomon offers to split the child into two pieces, one of them agrees but the other quickly relinquishes her claim. Solomon gives the boy to the latter.

"And Solomon's wisdom excelled the wisdom of all the children of the east country, and all the wisdom of Egypt. For he was wiser than all men. . . . And he spake three thousand proverbs: and his songs were a thousand and five." * [26]

As for his opulence, he has forty thousand stalls of horses, fourteen hundred chariots, a throne made of ivory overlaid with gold, golden drinking vessels, and golden shields. He makes "silver to be in Jerusalem as stones, and cedars made he to be as the sycamore trees that are in the vale, for abundance." In other words, gold is so plentiful that silver is considered of little value. (Modern archeological discoveries indicate, however, that copper mining was probably one of the main sources of Solomon's wealth. Control over copper districts intensified conflict between Israel and Edom.) He imports cedars from Lebanon, gold from Ophir, linen from Egypt, and ivory, apes, and peacocks from Tarsus. The point stressed by the historian is that Solomon's commerce extends to three continents: Asia, Africa, and Europe.

An effective climax to the summary of Solomon's splendor and wisdom is given in the famous account of the visit of the queen of Sheba.† Having heard much of his renown, this woman travels to Jerusalem to learn whether the tales she has heard have been accurate. Rich herself, she is not likely to be impressed by any ordinary display of wealth, but when she sees the house of Solomon (he has built his magnificent temple prior to her visit), the food on his table, the apparel of his attendants, and all the other

---

* This quotation helps to explain why the books of Proverbs and the Song of Songs have been traditionally attributed to Solomon. (There is no real evidence that he wrote either.)

† Sheba is a region in southwestern Arabia.

luxury with which he is surrounded, there is "no more spirit in her." She is equally astounded by his wisdom: there is no question which she can ask that he cannot answer.

Her summary of her admiration is eloquent: "It was a true report that I heard in mine own land of thy acts and of thy wisdom. Howbeit I believed not the words, until I came, and mine eyes had seen it: and, behold, the half was not told me: thy wisdom and prosperity exceedeth the fame which I heard."

THE BUILDING OF THE TEMPLE (I Kings 5–9). To the devout Hebrew historian, the building of the Temple at Jerusalem is an event of supreme importance. The Temple will centralize the worship of the Lord in one spot and will do away with the worship in local shrines—the "high places."

Now the Lord has promised David that his son would build the Temple. Solomon happily undertakes the task. He engages the services of Hiram, king of Tyre, who agrees to furnish the wood. Solomon conscripts an army of more than 180,000 workmen—stone-cutters, wood choppers, and burden bearers. After seven years of labor the Temple is finished. It is a large and elaborate structure, made chiefly of stone, cedar, and cypress, decorated with carvings of cherubim, of palm trees, and of flowers, covered with gold. (The plan and methods of building are believed to have been Phoenician, and similar walls with three rows of stone and cedar beams have been excavated in Syria). Solomon celebrates the completion of the Temple with a great festival, a sacrificial offering (of 22,000 oxen and 120,000 sheep), and a long prayer of dedication and blessing.

SOLOMON'S APOSTASY AND DEATH (I Kings 11). Although he is said to be incomparably wise and although he is a devout worshiper of the Lord, Solomon is guilty of great and foolish transgressions: he allows his wives to "turn away his heart after other gods." He has seven hundred wives and three hundred concubines. Many of these are foreigners, who persuade him to build altars and burn incense and offer sacrifices to such deities as Ashtoreth of the Sidonians, Milcom and Molech of the Ammonites, and Chemosh of the Moabites. The Lord tells Solomon that as a punishment the kingdom will be divided and most of it given to another line of kings. God punishes him further by inciting the kings of Edom and Syria to rebel against him. After reigning "forty" years, Solomon dies and is succeeded by his son Rehoboam.

The Divided Kingdom (I Kings 12—22). When the people convene to proclaim Rehoboam king, they petition him to lighten the burdens of taxation and forced labor which his father Solomon had placed on them. His wise old counselors warn him to do as the people request, but Rehoboam is induced to maintain and even to increase oppressive taxes by his rash young friends, who advise him to say to the people: "My little finger shall be thicker than my father's loins. And now whereas my father did lade you with a heavy yoke, I will add to your yoke: my father hath chastised you with whips, but I will chastise you with scorpions." *

In the meantime, Jeroboam, an exiled henchman of Solomon's who had once been in charge of the forced labor, has returned from Egypt. Now the ten northern tribes revolt against Rehoboam and choose Jeroboam as their king. The latter sets up his capital at Shechem; his kingdom is called "Israel." The tribes of Benjamin and Judah remain faithful to Rehoboam; his realm is known henceforth as "Judah."

POLITICAL EVENTS. The political history of both kingdoms (as told in I and II Kings) is presented in tabular form (pp. 112-115) and consequently requires only a brief summary here.

The kingdom of Judah continues under the Davidic dynasty during its entire existence as a nation, except for one brief interval (the reign of Athaliah, 842-837 B.C.). Twice it wages war against its sister kingdom Israel; and twice it allies itself with Israel against Syria. Edom gains its independence from Judah. In the eighth century B.C. under Ahaz and Hezekiah, the Southern Kingdom appeases Assyria by paying tribute. In the early years of the sixth century Judah becomes entangled in alliances with Egypt and thereby provokes Nebuchadrezzar of Babylon to overrun the country, to take many captives, and to burn Jerusalem (586 B.C.).

The political history of the Northern Kingdom is more turbulent than that of Judah. During its existence of 200 years, nineteen monarchs of nine different dynasties rule the land. Seven kings are assassinated. The capital is moved from Shechem to

---

* A "scorpion" probably referred to a scourge made of leather and spikes.

SOVEREIGNS OF THE SOUTHERN KINGDOM (JUDAH)

1. *Rehoboam* (922-915),[27] son of Solomon.* A "bad" king. I Kings 12 and 14:21-31.

2. *Abijam* (915-913). A "bad" king. I Kings 15:1-8.

3. *Asa* (913-873). A "good" king—destroys idols, forbids worship in local shrines, restores Temple treasures; wages war against Baasha, king of Israel. I Kings 15:9-24.

4. *Jehoshaphat* (873-849). On the whole a "good" king, but insufficiently zealous in prohibiting worship in local shrines. Joins King Ahab of Israel in ill-fated war against Syria. I Kings 22.

5. *Jehoram* (*Joram*) (849-842). A "bad" king—marries Athaliah, daughter of Ahab and Jezebel of Israel, and allows his kingdom to worship the gods of his in-laws. During his reign Edom successfully revolts against Judah. II Kings 8:16-24.

6. *Ahaziah* (842). A "bad" king—walks "in the way of the house of Ahab." He joins Israel in a war against Syria. He is killed in battle by Jehu. II Kings 8:25-29, 9:16-28.

7. *Athaliah* (842-837), daughter of Ahab and Jezebel, seizes throne on death of her son Ahaziah. A "bad" queen—kills most of "seed royal" of the Davidic line and tries to substitute Baal-worship for worship of the Lord. II Kings 11.

8. *Joash* (*Jehoash*) (837-800), grandson of Ahaziah and Athaliah, is restored to throne when Athaliah is deposed. A "good" king—repairs Temple in Jerusalem, but gives Temple treasures to king of Syria and fails to prohibit worship in local shrines. II Kings 12.

9. *Amaziah* (800-783). A "good" king, but one who still permits worship in "high places." II Kings 14:1-20.

10. *Azariah* (*Uzziah*) (783-742). A "good" king, but one who still does not abolish worship in local shrines. II Kings 14:21-22; 15:1-7.

11. *Jotham* (750-735). A "good" king, but one who still permits worship in local shrines. II Kings 15:32-38.

12. *Ahaz* (735-715). A "bad" king—worships at local shrines and burns his son as a sacrificial offering. Enlists aid of

* Except for Athaliah and Joash, each of the kings through Jehoahaz inherits the throne from his father.

SOVEREIGNS OF THE SOUTHERN KINGDOM (JUDAH)
(Continued)

Tiglath-pileser, king of Assyria, against the kings of Israel and Syria. Pays tribute to Assyria. II Kings 16.

13. *Hezekiah* (715-687). A "good" king—abolishes local shrines, defeats Philistines, and keeps Assyrians out of Judah. Associated with the prophet Isaiah. II Kings 18—20.

14. *Manasseh* (687-642). A "bad" king—worships Baal, practices magic, and sacrifices his son as a burnt offering. II Kings 21:1-18.

15. *Amon* (642-640). A "bad" king. II Kings 21:19-26.

16. *Josiah* (640-609). A very "good" king—repairs the Temple and brings about the great Deuteronomic reformation upon the discovery of the Book of Law in the Temple (621 B.C.). He destroys all the pagan shrines and altars, and he reinstitutes the observance of the old Jewish customs and festivals, such as the Passover. II Kings 22:1—23:30.

17. *Jehoahaz* (609). A "bad" king. Rules only three months (he is deposed by the king of Egypt). II Kings 23:31-34.

18. *Jehoiakim* (*Eliakim*) (609-598), son of Josiah, placed on throne by king of Egypt when Jehoahaz is dethroned. A "bad" king. He first pays tribute to Egypt, but then becomes vassal of Nebuchadrezzar of Babylon. He next rebels against Nebuchadrezzar and so provokes a war which is destined to have most disastrous consequences. II Kings 23:34—24:5.

19. *Jehoiachin* (598), son of Jehoiakim. A "bad" king. He continues the war against Babylon. Jerusalem falls (597), and many Hebrews (including Jehoiachin) are carried as exiles into Babylon. Later (561) Jehoiachin is freed from prison and given some privileges. II Kings 24:6-16, 25:27-30.

20. *Zedekiah* (*Mattaniah*) (598-587), uncle of Jehoiachin, placed on throne when Jehoiachin is deposed. A "bad" king. Like his predecessors, he rebels against Nebuchadrezzar, who again captures Jerusalem and burns it. Zedekiah's sons are killed, his eyes are put out, and a governor is appointed to rule the land. II Kings 24:17—25:22.

SOVEREIGNS OF THE NORTHERN KINGDOM (ISRAEL)

1. *Jeroboam I* (922-901), first ruler of the Northern Kingdom, chosen by the ten northern tribes as ruler when they revolt against Rehoboam of the southern tribes. A "bad" king—sets up golden calves for worship in Dan and Bethel and appoints priesthood not descended from Levi. Makes Shechem his capital. I Kings 12:12—14:20.

2. *Nadab* (901-300), son of Jeroboam I. A "bad" king. I Kings 14:20, 15:25-31.

3. *Baasha* (900-877), assassinates Nadab, establishes second dynasty. A "bad" king—idolatrous. Sets up capital at Tirzah. I Kings 15:27—16:7.

4. *Elah* (877-876), son of Baasha. A "bad" king. I Kings 16:8-10.

5. *Zimri* (876), an army officer, assassinates Elah, establishes the third "dynasty," which lasts only seven days. A "bad" king—idolatrous. I Kings 16:9-20.

6. *Omri* (876-869), commander of Elah's army, defeats and deposes Zimri, establishes fourth dynasty. A "bad," idolatrous king, but a strong one. He builds Samaria and makes it his capital. I Kings 16:16-28.

7. *Ahab* (869-850), son of Omri. A notoriously "bad" king—worships Baal. Husband of Sidonian princess Jezebel. He is the opponent of the prophet Elijah. Appropriates Naboth's vineyard. I Kings 16:29—22:40.

8. *Ahaziah* (850-849), son of Ahab. A "bad" king. Tries vainly to kill Elijah. I Kings 22:40, II Kings 1:1-18.

9. *Joram* (*Jehoram*) (849-842), son of Ahab. A "bad" king. He wages war successfully against Moab, unsuccessfully against Syria. Sometimes opponent of Elisha. II Kings 1:17—9:26.

10. *Jehu* (842-815), officer in the Israelitish army, anointed by Elisha, kills Joram and Jezebel and mounts throne, thus establishing the fifth dynasty. The first "good" king of Israel—destroys images and temples of Baal; but he does allow continuance of worship of golden calves set up by Jeroboam I. II Kings 9—10.

11. *Jehoahaz* (815-801), son of Jehu. A "bad" king. II Kings 13:1-9.

SOVEREIGNS OF THE NORTHERN KINGDOM (ISRAEL)
(*Continued*)

12. *Joash* (*Jehoash*) (801-786), son of Jehoahaz. A "bad" king. He wages war against Judah and sacks Jerusalem. II Kings 13:9—14:16.

13. *Jeroboam II* (786-746), son of Joash. A "bad" king, but Israel enjoys great prosperity during his reign. II Kings 14:23-29.

14. *Zachariah* (746-745), son of Jeroboam II. A "bad" king. II Kings 15:8-12.

15. *Shallum* (745), a conspirator, assassinates Zachariah and assumes throne, thus establishing the sixth dynasty, which lasts only a month. A "bad" king. II Kings 15:13-15.

16. *Menahem* (745-738), another conspirator, kills Shallum, takes throne, and sets up the seventh dynasty. A "bad" king. Pays tribute to Assyria to prevent ravaging of Israel. II Kings 15:14-22.

17. *Pekahiah* (738-736), son of Menahem. A "bad" king. II Kings 15:22-26.

18. *Pekah* (737-732), son of an army officer, assassinates Pekahiah and mounts throne, thus establishing the eighth dynasty. A "bad" king. During this reign the Assyrians under Tiglath-Pileser conquer part of Israel and take many captives into Assyria. II Kings 15:27-31.

19. *Hoshea* (732-724), a pro-Assyrian candidate for the crown, assassinates Pekah and takes the throne, thus establishing the ninth dynasty. A "bad" king. He conspires with Egypt against Assyria, which now overruns Israel and takes the inhabitants captive. Thus the Northern Kingdom comes to an end (722 B.C.). II Kings 17.

Tirzah and then to Samaria. In the first half of the ninth century a bond between Israel and Sidon is formed by the marriage of King Ahab to the Sidonian princess Jezebel. In addition to the two wars against Judah, Israel fights Moab and Syria. For a few years the Northern Kingdom staves off the Assyrian avalanche by paying tribute. About 734 B.C. Assyria conquers part of Israel and takes some captives. When King Hoshea makes an alliance with Egypt, the Assyrians complete the conquest of Israel and lead many more Israelites into exile (722 B.C.).

RELIGIOUS CONDITIONS. To the authors of the books of Kings, the religious conditions of the two kingdoms are fully as important as—and in large measure control—the political events.

In the Southern Kingdom the center of Yahweh-worship is, of course, the Temple in Jerusalem.* Worship at local shrines, such as groves and "high places," is, in the eyes of the Deuteronomic editors, an abominable practice, and the designation of each king of Judah as either "good" or "bad" depends primarily on whether he prohibits or condones such practice. Although Solomon and some of his successors are said to have worshiped idols and non-Hebrew deities, such worship is less widespread in the Southern Kingdom than in the Northern. Lacking a central temple, the people of the Northern Kingdom worship at various shrines of Yahweh, and furthermore, they are rather easily persuaded to shift their allegiance from Yahweh to foreign deities. The worship of false gods and the prevalence of social injustice and of personal immorality help occasion the rise of prophets, who, often in opposition to the royally appointed priests, exhort the people to return to the true God and to ethical behavior. Before the end of the eighth century the prophets interpret the threat of an Assyrian invasion as God's warning that he will use some alien power as an instrument to punish his Chosen People unless they reform. They refuse to reform, and hence—according to Biblical historians as well as the prophets—God subjects the people of both kingdoms to exile.

Jeroboam, Prototype of a "Wicked" King (I Kings 12—14). As soon as he establishes his capital in Shechem, Jeroboam sets up two golden calves as objects of worship, representative of Yahweh "as the God of physical forces." [28] Worship at these two shrines is considered by the Deuteronomic compilers to be apostasy to the Lord. Matters are made worse by Jeroboam's appointment of a priesthood not derived from the house of Levi. Despite the protests of an unnamed "man of God" and despite the withering of his own hand (sent by God as a punishment for his apostasy), Jeroboam persists in his evil ways. The historian is particularly bitter about Jeroboam's wickedness and seems to feel that this king is in large measure responsible for Israel's future apostasy;

* Emphasis by the priests on Temple worship in Jerusalem after the return from Babylon helps to explain why the Southern Kingdom takes pre-eminence over the Northern in post-Exilic writings.

time after time the books of Kings use such phrases as "walking in the way of Jeroboam and in his sin which he did, to make Israel to sin." [29]

Ahab, Israel's Most "Wicked" King (I Kings 16:29—22:40). According to the author of I Kings 16, Ahab, the son of the strong king Omri, does more to provoke the Lord to anger than had all the kings of Israel who formerly reigned. Not only does he follow the idolatrous ways of Jeroboam, but also he marries the Sidonian (Phoenician) princess Jezebel,* who persuades him to worship Baal † and to build altars to him. Repeatedly Ahab is warned by the prophet Elijah to mend his ways and to worship God, but the king obstinately refuses to obey.

Ahab leads his country in two wars against Syria (Ch. 20). For a long time, apparently, Ahab has been a vassal of Ben-hadad, the Syrian king. Now Ben-hadad besieges Samaria, Ahab's capital, reduces its garrison to a desperate state, and demands its complete capitulation, including the surrender of the silver, the gold, and the wives and the children of Ahab. Ahab agrees; but when Ben-hadad insultingly orders him to allow Syrian servants to search his house and take anything they please, Ahab (after a conference with his subjects) decides to resist. A small body of Israelites takes the overconfident Syrians completely by surprise, throws them into a panic, and then, with the aid of several thou-

---

* There is an unproven theory that Psalm 45 was originally written to celebrate the marriage of Ahab and Jezebel. If the theory is correct, then perhaps the contemporary court Psalmist did not agree with the Deuteronomic historian that Ahab was a wicked king. It is interesting to note that the author of I Kings 20:1-34 is more favorable to Ahab than is the historian responsible for the other passages which concern this king. These differences of opinion are a good reminder that the Bible is a complicated collection of writings by different authors in different ages. See Norman H. Snaith, exegesis to II Kings, *The Interpreter's Bible*, III, 166.

Some commentators call Jezebel a Tyrian princess rather than a Sidonian. Both Tyre and Sidon were cities in Phoenicia.

† The Hebrew word *baal* (plural, *baals* or *baalim*) means "lord" or "master." The baalim were local nature deities of the Canaanites. The singular *Baal* is used by the compilers of I Kings to refer to Melkart, the chief male deity of the Phoenicians. In Israel under Ahab and Jezebel, there was some fusion of Canaanite baalism and the Tyrian cult of Melkart. See D. C. Simpson, commentary on I and II Kings, *The Abingdon Bible Commentary*, ed. by Frederick Carl Eiselen, Edwin Lewis, and David G. Downey (New York: Abingdon-Cokesbury Press, 1929), p. 426.

CYPRUS

The Great Sea

PHOENICIA

Sidon

Tyre

Mt. LEBANON

ARAM (SYRIA)

Damascus

Megiddo

KINGDOM OF ISRAEL

R. Jordan

Samaria

Joppa

Bethel

PHILISTIA

Jerusalem

Tekoa

Dead Sea

Gaza

AMMON

MOAB

KINGDOM
OF
JUDAH

EDOM

(ARABIAN DESERT)

N

SCALE OF MILES
0 10   60

DIVIDED KINGDOM
(ca. 860 B.C.)

From *A Handbook for Know Your Bible Study Groups*, © 1959 by Abingdon Press. By permission of the publisher.

sand more Israelites, wins a crushing victory. The Syrians claim
that they have been defeated because the Israelites' God is a
deity of the hills and not of the plains; therefore they muster another army and meet Ahab's men again, this time on level ground.
Because the Syrians have belittled his power, the Lord punishes
them by allowing the Israelites to defeat them again—so deci-
sively that Israel frees itself of vassalage. Ben-hadad himself is
captured but is mercifully set free by Ahab. In a passage (I Kings
20:35-43) written by an author inimical to Ahab, a prophet
predicts disaster for this king for making peace with the Syrians
instead of destroying them utterly.

After three years of friendly relations with Syria, Ahab decides
to seize some disputed territory held by the Syrians (I Kings
22:1). He and Jehoshaphat, the king of Judah, form an alliance
and begin preparing for war. As is his custom, Ahab invites four
hundred prophets—"men of God," not prophets of Baal—to ask
whether he should attack the Syrian forces; all these prophets
encourage him to proceed with the invasion, and one, named
Zedekiah, even exhibits some iron horns to symbolize how Syria
will be gored. There is, however, another prophet, Micaiah, who
has not been consulted because he has a reputation for foretell-
ing evil.* When Jehoshaphat insists on hearing what Micaiah has
to say about the matter, that prophet lies at first and predicts
success for Israel, because he is afraid that he will be punished
if he again foretells disaster.† Ahab, however, apparently senses
that Micaiah is lying and therefore urges him to tell the truth.
Thereupon the prophet predicts disaster for the expedition and
death for Ahab; furthermore, he reveals why the four hundred
prophets have predicted falsely: when God was seeking a way to
bring about Ahab's downfall, one of his spirits volunteered to be
a "lying spirit" in the mouths of the four hundred, and God accepted the offer. (Thus the Biblical author intimates that God
sometimes uses devious means to motivate human conduct.)

* The failure to invite to a gathering someone of ill omen is perhaps a
folk element which has crept into the Biblical story. Compare the slights to
(1) the wicked witch in the story of the Sleeping Beauty and (2) the
goddess Eris (Discord) in the Greek myth about the marriage of Peleus
and Thetis.

† Compare Calchas' reluctance to tell Agamemnon the cause of the
plague on the Greeks at the opening of the *Iliad*.

When Zedekiah hears Micaiah's oracles, he angrily strikes his rival on the cheek and asks: "Which way went the Spirit of the Lord from me to speak unto thee?" Micaiah replies that Zedekiah will receive the answer to that question when hiding (presumably from the Syrians) in his inner chamber.

Believing the predictions of the four hundred prophets, Ahab throws the lone dissenter Micaiah into prison and continues with preparations for the battle. But perhaps he has been shaken by Micaiah's prophecy, for he disguises himself as a common soldier. Despite this precaution, he is killed by a random arrow. His blood flows into his chariot, which is later washed in a pool of Samaria. Some dogs lick up this blood in the pool, and thus is fulfilled an old prophecy made by Elijah (see below, p. 124).

Jezebel, Prototype of a "Wicked Woman" (I Kings 16:31, 18:4, 19:1-3, 21:5-25; II Kings 9:30-37). Although relatively few verses of the Bible are concerned with Jezebel, the wife of Ahab, so great is her reputation for evil that her name has become a common noun, a synonym for a "wicked woman." Not only does she reintroduce Baal-worship into Israel, but she "stirs up" her husband to act with all the despotism and cruelty of the average Oriental monarch of the era. Furthermore, she banishes the prophets of the Lord and replaces them with 450 prophets of Baal and 400 prophets of the groves (local shrines). After Elijah discredits and destroys her prophets (I Kings 18:17-40), she sends him a message of the most violent hatred: "So let the gods do to me, and more also, if I make not thy life as the life of one of them by to-morrow about this time." She is unable, however, to carry out her threat because Elijah escapes into Judah. One of her worst crimes is the instigation of the cold-blooded murder of Naboth; for this Elijah prophesies that the "dogs shall eat Jezebel by the wall of Jezreel" (I Kings 21:23).

When the conspirator Jehu kills her son, King Joram,* Jezebel knows that her death, too, is imminent. She takes great pains to beautify herself, painting her face and adorning her head.[30] As Jehu enters the gates of Jezreel, she mocks him from her window, comparing him with Zimri, who had gained the throne for seven days by murdering his master. Jehu persuades Jezebel's servants to throw her out the window; then his horses trample her to death. Somewhat later he remembers that she is a king's

* See below, p. 121.

daughter and therefore deserves a decent burial, but when his servants return to inter her body, they find only her skull, her feet, and the palms of her hands; all else has been devoured by the ferocious dogs which roam the streets of Jezreel. Thus is fulfilled Elijah's prophecy of Jezebel's fate.

Jehu's Conspiracy (II Kings 9—10). During the reign of Joram (Jehoram), who is one of Ahab's sons, the prophet Elisha * stirs up a revolution which is destined to put an end to the "wicked" dynasty of Omri (the father of Ahab). While Israel is at war with Syria, Elisha sends a disciple to anoint Jehu, a captain in the Israelitish army, as king of Israel. Jehu wastes no time in implementing his nomination. He drives furiously † to Jezreel, where Joram, who is recuperating from a battle wound, drives in a chariot to meet him. "Is it peace, Jehu?" Joram asks hopefully. Jehu replies that there can be no peace while the land is so full of idolatry. Joram flees, but Jehu pursues him, kills him, and (as an act of retributive justice) throws his body into Naboth's vineyard.†† The people proclaim Jehu king.

The new sovereign promptly proceeds to obliterate the house of Ahab. At his direction the elders of Samaria and Jezreel kill all seventy of Ahab's surviving sons and send their heads to him. Next he lures all the prophets of Baal into their temple, where he has them slain; he breaks and burns the sacred pillars and converts the temple into a latrine. Thus he wipes out the worship of Baal in Israel. The Lord rewards him by promising that his descendants "unto the fourth generation" will rule the kingdom. But Jehu allows the people to continue to worship the two golden calves which Jeroboam set up in Bethel and Dan and to which the people offered sacrifices as if to gods; therefore he is punished by having to fight continually against the Syrians, who harass the land and take all of Israel east of the Jordan.

The Elijah Cycle (I Kings 17—19, 21; II Kings 1:1-17). The prophet Elijah plays so important a role in the drama of Israel that it has been necessary to mention him frequently in the foregoing accounts. Comparable to Samuel as God's agent for select-

* See below, pp. 125-127, the discussion of the cycle of stories about Elisha.

† The furious driving of Jehu has become proverbial, and the common noun *jehu* denotes (in slang) a reckless or fast driver.

†† See below, p. 124.

ing and rejecting kings, Elijah's political influence in his own day was considerable. He was, furthermore, a forerunnner of Amos as a stern and vociferous critic of the paganism and the social injustice rampant in the Northern Kingdom. He left so deep an impression on the Hebrew people that a large number of traditions grew up about his name: Malachi, for instance, prophesied that it would be Elijah who would announce the coming of the Messiah (Mal. 4:5); in New Testament times the priests and Levites of Jerusalem were anxious to learn whether Elijah had been reincarnated in John the Baptist (John 1:21); Elijah appeared with Moses at the Transfiguration of Christ (Matt. 17:3, Mark 9:4, Luke 9:30); and even today some orthodox Jews set a chair for him at the rite of circumcision and leave a door "ajar for his entrance at Passover." [31]

The Elijah cycle is based on a series of tales from the Northern Kingdom, written perhaps as early as 800 B.C. The cycle bears evidence of an oral transmission over a rather long period: it relates several events which may be considered legendary (such as the ravens' feeding of Elijah), and it reflects the popular admiration for the heroic prophet who dared to stand up for God in defiance of the rulers of Israel. In I and II Kings the stories about Elijah are told with great enthusiasm. Full of vivid pictorial details and dramatic crises, they are "among the most brilliant and charming in Hebrew literature and their author an accomplished teller of tales." [32]

PROPHECY OF DROUGHT (I Kings 17). The abruptness with which the historian introduces Elijah helps to convey an impression of the "suddenness" [33] and unpredictability of the intrepid old prophet: "And Elijah the Tishbite, who was of the inhabitants of Gilead, said unto Ahab, As the Lord God of Israel liveth, before whom I stand, there shall not be dew nor rain these years, but according to my word." To escape Ahab's anger, Elijah flees to an uninhabited region, where ravens bring him food and where he drinks from a brook. When the brook dries up, he goes into a city and seeks food and drink from a poor widow, whose plea of poverty is piteous: "As the Lord thy God liveth, I have not a cake, but an handful of meal in a barrel, and a little oil in a cruse: and, behold, I am gathering two sticks, that I may go in and dress it for me and my son, that we may eat it, and die" (I Kings 17:12). Elijah promises her aid if she will feed him. She consents, and he miraculously causes her meal barrel and oil cruse never to become empty thereafter, "until the day that the Lord sendeth rain upon the earth." He performs another miracle in reviving her dead son.

THE CONTEST AT MOUNT CARMEL (I Kings 18). In the third year of the drought and famine, in obedience to God's command Elijah goes back to see Ahab in Samaria. As soon as the king beholds him, he accuses the prophet: "Art thou he that troubleth Israel?" Fearlessly Elijah replies, "I have not troubled Israel; but thou, and thy father's house, in that ye have forsaken the commandments of the Lord, and thou hast followed Baalim." Then he orders Ahab to assemble at Mount Carmel all the people of Israel, the 450 prophets of Baal, and the 400 prophets of the groves. When they have all gathered, Elijah confronts the people with a disturbing question: "How long halt ye between two opinions? If the Lord be God, follow him: but if Baal, then follow him." The people are unable to answer a word.

Next Elijah challenges the pagan prophets to a contest. The prophets are to prepare one sacrifice and Elijah to prepare another. Each side will then call on its deity to send fire to consume its sacrifice. The prophets accept the challenge. They pray to Baal "from morning even until noon," but nothing happens to the bullock which they have cut up on their altar. Elijah mocks them: "Cry aloud: for he is a god; either he is talking, or he is pursuing, or he is in a journey, or peradventure he sleepeth, and must be awaked." The prophets leap on their altar, cry aloud, and even cut themselves with knives, but still there is no answer. Now Elijah prepares his altar. Fire falls upon the sacrificial offering and consumes not only the bullock but also the altar itself and even the stones and the dust. The people are converted and fall on their faces and cry out: "The Lord, he is the God!" At Elijah's direction they slay all the prophets of Baal. Finally Elijah says that the drought is at an end, he and Ahab go to Jezreel, and soon rain falls plentifully on Israel.

SECOND EXILE AND THE ANOINTING OF ELISHA (I Kings 19). Fleeing again (this time to escape the wrath of Jezebel), Elijah goes to a wilderness in southern Judah. There he prays for his own death. An angel brings him bread and water. A very memorable scene follows. The Lord tells him to go up on a mountain and to stand there before the Lord. "And, behold, the Lord passed by, and a great and strong wind rent the mountains, and brake in pieces the rocks before the Lord; but the Lord was not in the wind: and after the wind an earthquake; but the Lord was not in the earthquake: And after the earthquake a fire; but the Lord was not in the fire: and after the fire a still small voice." This is the voice of the Lord. It tells him to go back north and to anoint Hazael to be king of Syria, Jehu to be king of Israel, and Elisha to be Elijah's own successor as a prophet. Elijah obeys the "still small voice" and sets out. En route he encounters Elisha and casts his mantle upon him as a token of discipleship. Elisha follows the prophet to Israel.

NABOTH'S VINEYARD (I Kings 21). In the town of Jezreel near Samaria a man named Naboth owns an excellent vineyard, which Ahab covets. He offers Naboth either another vineyard or money, but Naboth (who regards the property as a family heritage which cannot rightfully be sold) refuses each offer. Perceiving her husband's disappointment, Jezebel tells Ahab that she will procure the vineyard for him and sends two false witnesses to Jezreel to proclaim that Naboth has blasphemed God and the king and incite the people to stone him to death. As soon as Ahab hears that Naboth is dead, he takes possession of the coveted vineyard. Then the Lord sends Elijah to say to Ahab: "Thus saith the Lord, In the place where dogs licked the blood of Naboth shall dogs lick thy blood, even thine." In despair, Ahab cries out to Elijah: "Hast thou found me, O mine enemy?" Elijah foretells that all Ahab's male descendants will be slain and that dogs will eat the body of Jezebel by the wall of Jezreel.

RELATIONS WITH AHAZIAH (II Kings 1:1-15). Upon the death of Ahab, the king's son Ahaziah ascends the throne of Israel. Like his father and his mother, Ahaziah is an idolater and a worshiper of Baal. After ruling only two years, he is injured by a fall. He sends messengers to inquire of Baal-zebub, the god of Ekron, whether he will recover. Deploring the king's consulting of a foreign god instead of Yahweh, Elijah intercepts the messengers and sends them back to Ahaziah. Three times the king dispatches soldiers to arrest the prophet, who twice calls down heavenly fire upon the soldiers (the third time the leader of the soldiers begs Elijah for mercy) and then visits the king and prophesies his early death. Ahaziah dies soon after that.

THE ASCENSION OF ELIJAH (II Kings 2:1-15). Several years later, Elijah knows that it is time for him to depart this world.

Together he and Elisha walk to the banks of the Jordan River. Elijah parts the waters by striking them with his mantle,* and the two prophets cross to the other side. Elijah asks his companion what boon he would like to be granted; Elisha replies with the famous words: "I pray thee, let a double portion of thy spirit be upon me." Soon they behold a chariot of fire and horses of fire, and a whirlwind carries Elijah up into heaven. His mantle symbolically falls on Elisha, who parts the Jordan again with the garment and sadly returns to Jericho.

The Elisha Cycle (II Kings 2—9, 13:14-21). As a prophet, Elisha is somewhat less impressive and less admirable than Elijah. Whereas the latter seems to be interested primarily in religion and righteous conduct and to be remote and aloof, appearing suddenly at moments of crisis, Elisha is greatly concerned with political matters, and he is ubiquitous—always on hand to participate in whatever is going on. Although he is zealous in helping those who serve the Lord, Elisha is sometimes cruel and bloodthirsty; witness his instigation of Jehu's plot against the whole family of Ahab.

Furthermore, the Elisha cycle has less literary merit than the stories about Elijah; it is less organically unified and "more filled with the miraculous and the legendary." [34]

SEVEN MIRACLES OF ASSISTANCE (II Kings 2:19-22; 3:11-20; 4:1-44; and 6:1-7). As Elijah's successor, Elisha immediately begins to perform miracles, usually to help people in distress.

Four of these marvels are concerned with providing or purifying food or drink. One of his first acts is to aid the men of Jericho, whose water supply is bad and whose land is barren; Elisha "heals" the water by casting salt into it. On another occasion the combined armies of Israel, Edom, and Judah, which are waging war against Moab, find that their water supply is exhausted. Elisha orders the Israelites to dig many ditches; these he causes to fill up with water. In Gilgal he purifies some poison pottage by throwing meal into it. And at another time he causes twenty loaves of barley and a sack of corn to increase so as to be sufficient to feed a hundred men.

The similarity of two of Elisha's miracles to deeds performed by Elijah suggests that these later stories are in reality "doublets," or borrowings from the earlier cycle—a suggestion which

---

* Compare Moses' parting of the Red Sea (Ex. 14:21) and Joshua's dividing of the waters of the Jordan (Jos. 3:15-16).

gains weight when one considers how nearly alike the names of the prophets are. In the first of these two tales about Elisha, he miraculously increases a poor widow's supply of oil. In the second, he raises a young boy from the dead.

A seventh miracle of assistance is making an iron axe head (which has fallen into the Jordan) rise and float.

CURSING THE CHILDREN (II Kings 2:23-25). Once as Elisha is leaving Jericho, some children rudely make fun of him, shouting: "Go up, thou bald head; go up, thou bald head." Elisha curses them in the name of the Lord, and two she-bears come out of the forest and tear forty-two of the children. This story, shocking to modern readers, is probably told to inculcate respect for prophets.

NAAMAN'S LEPROSY (II Kings 5). The most skillfully told of all the stories about Elisha is that concerning Naaman, commander of the Syrian army, who has leprosy. Naaman's little maidservant, an Israelitish captive, grieves over her master's illness and tells him that a prophet in Samaria could cure him. Naaman goes to Samaria, bearing with him many valuable presents— gold, silver, and ten festal garments. First he calls upon the king and asks to be cured. Joram rends his own clothes and asks in despair: "Am I God, to kill and to make alive, that his man doth send unto me to recover a man of his leprosy?" When Elisha hears about the king's predicament, he sends for Naaman and tells him to wash himself seven times in the river Jordan. Naaman is angry that the cure should be so simple and asks: "Are not Abana and Pharpar, rivers of Damascus, better than all the waters of Israel?" His servants persuade him, however, to try the prophet's prescription. The malady disappears—his flesh becomes clean "like unto the flesh of a little child." The miracle convinces him that the Lord is the only God. Filled with gratitude, he urges Elisha to accept the gifts which he has brought from Syria, but Elisha refuses them. Then Naaman asks two more favors: first, that he be allowed to carry back to Syria some Israelitish earth on which to worship the Lord—apparently because he feels that Yahweh cannot be worshiped except on such soil; [35] and second, that he be forgiven in the future for accompanying his master into the temple of the god Rimmon and appearing to worship the false deity. Elisha grants his requests: "Go in peace."

After Naaman's departure, Gehazi, the servant of Elisha, yearns for some of the dazzling gifts which his master has refused. He overtakes Naaman and says that Elisha has reconsidered and would like a talent of silver and two changes of garments. Naaman insists that he take two talents with the garments, and Gehazi accepts. When Gehazi returns, Elisha asks where he has been. The servant lies: "Thy servant went no whither." Then Elisha rebukes him for lying and for being avaricious, and as a punishment causes him to be smitten with Naaman's leprosy. This is a moral tale showing the evils of greed. The smiting of Gehazi with the very leprosy of Naaman is a typical folk element—the "punishment fits the crime."

THE CONFOUNDING OF THE SYRIANS (II Kings 6—7). The Syrians and the Israelites are at war with each other once again. Ben-hadad of Syria suspects the presence of spies in his army, because all his maneuvers seem to be known beforehand by the Israelites. When told that Elisha can divine his secret counsels and report them to the king of Israel, Ben-hadad sends a great host to capture the prophet. Elisha's servant becomes terrified, but Elisha "opens his eyes" and enables him to see the encircling mountains full of heaven-sent horses and chariots of fire. Then the prophet causes blindness to fall on all Ben-hadad's men, and he leads them to Samaria, pretending that he is taking them where they can capture Elisha. In Samaria he restores their sight and causes King Joram to let them go peacefully back to Syria.

After a brief truce, war begins again, and the Syrians besiege Samaria so that terrible famine comes to the city. The Israelites are reduced to eating asses' heads, doves' dung, and even their own children. Accused of causing the disaster, Elisha prophesies that the famine will be ended immediately. The Lord makes the Syrian army hear a noise like the roaring of a great host of horses and chariots. Believing themselves to be under attack by the Egyptians and the Hittites, the Syrians flee in panic, leaving their food and equipment behind them. The Samarians rush out to seize the abandoned supplies, and the famine is ended.

Athaliah's Usurpation of the Throne of Judah (II Kings 11:1-21). In the Southern Kingdom, Athaliah, the daughter of Ahab and Jezebel, hearing that her son Ahaziah is dead, assumes the throne and tries to wipe out all the descendants of King David in order to strengthen her own position as sovereign. She succeeds in killing all the "seed royal" of the house of Judah except the one-year-old Joash (Jehoash), the son of Ahaziah. This child is saved by Jehosheba, the sister of Ahaziah, who at first hides him in her own bedchamber; then she and Jehoiada * the priest hide the lad in the Temple for six years. At the propitious moment Jehoiada gathers a considerable group of soldiers, shows Joash to them, and persuades them to swear allegiance to him. The priest anoints and crowns the young prince, and the people clap their hands and shout: "God save the king." When Athaliah hears the trumpets blowing and the people rejoicing, she tears her clothes † and cries: "Treason! Treason!" But Jehoiada's men seize her and kill her with the sword. Thereafter the people destroy the temple, altars, and images of Baal and slay Baal's priest.

Hezekiah, a Virtuous but Foolish King (II Kings 18–20). Events of great importance take place in the Southern Kingdom during the reign of Hezekiah, the son of Ahaz.

REFORM (II Kings 18:1-12). King Hezekiah is very different from his sinful and idolatrous father. Not only does he worship the Lord, but he removes the high places, breaks the images, cuts down the groves, and even destroys the brazen serpent supposedly handed down from Moses—a serpent to which the people are accustomed to burn incense. For these reforms God gives Hezekiah victory over the Philistines and (for a while) freedom from the Assyrians.

THE DESTRUCTION OF SENNACHERIB (II Kings 18:13–19:37). Sennacherib, the king of Assyria, captures many fortified cities of Judah, and Hezekiah himself sends tribute—treasures from his own house and from the house of the Lord. Then Sennacherib accuses Hezekiah of trying to enlist the aid of the king of Egypt, whom the Assyrian scoffingly refers to as a "bruised reed." Sennacherib demands more tribute. Next we are introduced to the prophet Isaiah, who is violently opposed to an alliance with Egypt and who delivers God's messages to Hezekiah. The king of Judah seeks Isaiah's advice about increasing the

---

* The book of II Chronicles (22:11), followed by Racine in *Athaliah*, makes Jehosheba the wife of Jehoiada.

† The tearing of one's clothes was an impressive gesture indicative of distress. Jacob, for example, rends his garments when he is told that Joseph has been killed by a wild beast (Gen. 37:34).

tribute to Sennacherib. In a famous "taunt song" delivered to Hezekiah by Isaiah, God promises to defeat the blasphemous Assyrians (II Kings 19:21-28) and to save Jerusalem for the time being. That night a terrible plague ("the angel of the Lord") smites Sennacherib's men and kills 185,000: ". . . and when they arose early in the morning, behold, they were all dead corpses." Sennacherib returns to Nineveh and is murdered by his own sons soon thereafter.

FOLLY (II Kings 20:12-19). By this time Babylon has become a great power in the Orient. Baladin, the king of Babylon, sends his son with letters and a gift for Hezekiah. Most unwisely, the king of Judah shows the young man all his treasures—"the silver, and the gold, and the spices, and the precious ointment, and all the house of his armour, and all that was found in his treasures: there was nothing in his house, nor in all his dominion, that Hezekiah shewed them not." When Isaiah hears about this foolish act of vanity, he makes a dire prediction: "Behold, the days come, that all that is in thine house, and that which thy fathers have laid up in store unto this day, shall be carried into Babylon: nothing shall be left, saith the Lord." Hezekiah seems undisturbed by this prophecy, so long as he will have peace in his day.

Josiah and Deuteronomic Reform in the Southern Kingdom (II Kings 22:1—23:30).[36] After the reigns of the "wicked" kings Manasseh and Amon, the "good" king Josiah succeeds to the throne of Judah. He does that which is right in the sight of the Lord and walks in all the ways of David, turning not aside to the right hand or to the left. He also repairs the Temple.

By far the most important event during his reign is the high priest Hilkiah's discovery of the lawbook in the Temple.* When Josiah reads this book and considers how its laws have been ignored by the people of Judah, he is so alarmed that he rends his clothes and commands Hilkiah and others: "Go ye, enquire of the Lord for me, and for the people, and for all Judah, concerning the words of this book that is found: for great is the wrath of the Lord that is kindled against us, because our fathers have not hearkened unto the words of this book, to do according unto all that which is written concerning us." He assembles

* See above, p. 45, for the discussion of the D Document, believed to be based on this book discovered by Hilkiah.

all the people to hear the lawbook read. Then follows the great Deuteronomic reformation (621 B.C.). Once again all the pagan shrines, altars, and images over the entire kingdom are destroyed, and their priests are either killed or suppressed. Wizards and magicians are "put away." Of great importance is the reinstitution of the observance of the Passover. The historian gives Josiah the highest accolade: "And like unto him was there no king before him, that turned to the Lord with all his heart, and with all his soul, and with all his might, according to all the law of Moses; neither after him arose there any like him."

Josiah meets an untimely end (c. 609 or 608 B.C.) in an expedition against an Egyptian king who is leading a raid on Assyria.

End of Monarchy and National Independence (II Kings 23:31 —25:30). The history of the reigns of the last four kings of Judah is made up of accounts of one catastrophe after another. During Josiah's reign a prophetess has foretold that after Josiah's time the Lord will punish the people of Judah for their sins. Punishment now threatens in the form of military invasion—by Babylon from the north and by Egypt from the south.

Jehoahaz, the son of Josiah, is taken captive by Pharaoh of Egypt, who dethrones him and places Eliakim, another of Josiah's sons, on the throne. At first Eliakim (whose name Pharaoh changes to Jehoiakim) pays tribute regularly. But then he becomes a vassal of Nebuchadrezzar, king of Babylon. After three years he rebels against Babylon, and so Nebuchadrezzar makes war against him. The Babylonians are joined by bands of Syrians, Moabites, and Ammonites, the ancient foes of the Jewish people. "Surely," says the historian, "at the commandment of the Lord came this upon Judah, to remove them out of his sight, for the sins of Manasseh, according to all that he did."

While the war is still going on, Jehoiakim (who has ruled eleven years) dies and is succeeded by his son Jehoiachin. This king also does evil in the sight of the Lord. In the eighth year (597 B.C.) of his reign, therefore, the Lord allows Nebuchadrezzar to take Jerusalem and to send 10,000 inhabitants of the country (including Jehoiachin) to Babylon as captives.

Nebuchadrezzar gives the Hebrews one more chance. He makes Mattaniah, Josiah's son, king of Judah and changes his name to Zedekiah. Zedekiah, however, is sinful, and the Lord causes him to rebel unsuccessfully against Nebuchadrezzar. Now

Nebuchadrezzar's patience is exhausted; he besieges Jerusalem and burns it to the ground, including the Lord's Temple. After killing Zedekiah's two sons in the presence of their father, Nebuchadrezzar puts out Zedekiah's eyes and appoints Gedaliah, a Hebrew, governor of the land. Seven months later the people revolt, kill the governor, and flee to Egypt. Thus the kingdom of Judah comes to an end.

A note of hope is preserved in a sort of postscript. The historian mentions that in the thirty-seventh year of Jehoiachin's captivity, Evil-merodach, the new king of Babylon, frees the Jewish monarch from prison, allows him to eat at the king's own table, and gives him an annuity for the remainder of his life.

5

Establishment of a Church State
after the Exile:
I and II Chronicles, Ezra, Nehemiah, and I Esdras

After the fall of Jerusalem to the Babylonians in 586 B.C., the "desolation of Judah was practically complete." [1] The Temple was burned, and the walls of the capital city were flattened. An estimated 27,000 Hebrews were deported; a few others escaped into Egypt. Apparently only a handful of small farmers and herdsmen remained in what had once been the Southern Kingdom.

The ten tribes of the kingdom of Israel who had been led into exile by the Assyrians in 721 B.C. had become "lost"; that is, they had been scattered over Asia Minor and had ceased to exist as a racial unit. But the two Southern tribes, Benjamin and Judah, refused to be absorbed by their captors and struggled valiantly (by payment of tribute to Assyria when necessary to save the tribes) to preserve their worship of Yahweh, the strongest bond which held them together. Nebuchadrezzar, king of Babylonia, destroyed Jerusalem and exiled the people of Judah in 586 B.C. In exile (586-536 B.C.) they originated worship in the synagogue, a practice which has been followed ever since that time by Jews living outside of Palestine; and they continued their writing of law, history, and prophecy.

It appears that Nebuchadrezzar treated the Hebrews with some degree of leniency but that his successors, Nabunaid and Belshazzar, were rather oppressive. At any rate, the exiles welcomed Cyrus of Persia as a deliverer when he conquered Babylon in 538 B.C.; he issued an edict permitting them to return to their own country. A band of Jews, led by one Sheshbazzar, made plans to take advantage of Cyrus' offer, but little seems to have been accomplished till about 520-516 B.C., when another group, under Zerubbabel, a descendant of Jehoiachin, returned to Jerusalem, built a makeshift Temple, and recommenced the ancient ceremonies of worship.

History is silent concerning the Jews in Palestine for the following seventy-two years. Then in 444 B.C. the Persian king (probably Artaxerxes II) authorized Nehemiah to rebuild the walls of Jerusalem. Early in the fourth century B.C. the priest Ezra brought about 1,800 Hebrews back to the city and effected some religious reforms.

The Jews were granted a large degree of autonomy as long as they remained under Persian rule.

I AND II CHRONICLES: A RE-EVALUATION OF ANCIENT JEWISH HISTORY

In the original Hebrew, I and II Chronicles were a single book. The Hebrew name for this book was *Dibhre Hayyamin,* meaning "annals." [2] The compilers of the Septuagint divided this work into two books and gave them the title *Paraleopomena,* meaning "things omitted" (that is, things left out of the books of Samuel and Kings). St. Jerome used the word *Chronicon* (an approximation of the Hebrew title), from which the English name of the books is derived.

For a long time there has been—and there still is—much scholarly disagreement about the authorship and the date of the two books of Chronicles.[3] Some scholars assert categorically that Ezra was the author and that he wrote the books about 380-350 B.C. Other commentators have vigorously maintained that the books were written much later, perhaps as late as 250 B.C., and that the identity of the author is unknown. The majority opinion appears to be that I and II Chronicles, Ezra, and Nehemiah were all written by the same person (but not Ezra), probably a Levite, and that the books of Chronicles were composed between 332 and 250 B.C. The author is called "the Chronicler."

The books of Chronicles are not history in the present-day sense of the term or even in the sense that Samuel and Kings are history. The Chronicler had no intention of writing an authentic and systematic record of events; *that* had already been done adequately in the Hexateuch, Judges, Samuel, and Kings.

Instead, the author intended to present so selective and so idealized a narrative that his contemporaries would not mistake it
for real history but would plainly recognize the sermonic purposes for which it was written.

In order to understand the sermonic thesis, one needs to recall
the status of the Jewish people. Although their dream of national
glory had been shattered, some of them had returned from exile
and had re-established the worship of Yahweh in Jerusalem. By
the middle of the fourth century B.C., however, the priests had
apparently become indolent in their duties and the people apa-
thetic in their worship. Against these tendencies the Chronicler
took his stand. His purposes were to recall the priests and Levites
to a more zealous performance of their official functions, to inspire in the people a greater devotion to God, and to stress the
importance of Temple worship in Jerusalem according to the
ancient book of laws.

His method is to idealize the "good old days," the glorious
times of David and Solomon, and then to demonstrate the evils
which befell the kingdoms when the later kings and the people
ceased to worship God and obey his commandments. David is
emphasized as a religious leader rather than a great political
and military figure, and he is given credit for establishing the
entire system of Temple worship and for introducing music into
the religious ceremonies. The stories in I and II Samuel which
are detrimental to his character (notably the Bathsheba episode)
are omitted. Since the Chronicler is primarily interested in
Temple worship, he restricts his narrative almost entirely to the
events in Jerusalem and the kingdom of Judah.

Both books of Chronicles have usually been considered less
distinguished literature than Samuel and Kings. In the first place,
they are repetitions of parts of those earlier books of history and
have little real information to add. In the second place, they
omit many of the "human interest" stories found in the older
books, such as the charming account of Samuel's birth and childhood and the stories about Elijah. In the third place, the books
of Chronicles contain many inaccuracies, exaggerations, and inconsistencies; for example, Jehoshaphat is said to have 1,160,000
soldiers in Jerusalem. The chief literary value of the books lies
in the Chronicler's ability to share his own earnest devotion
with his readers and in his addition of a few idyllic and lyrical
passages which do not appear in Samuel or Kings.

Genealogical Survey of History from Adam to David (I Chr. 1–9).[4] The first nine chapters of I Chronicles trace the ancestry of the Israelites and their relatives. Chapter 1 takes us from Adam through the sons of Esau. Chapters 2–9 are devoted to the genealogies of the twelve tribes of Israel, including the "half-tribes" of Manasseh and Ephraim. Special attention is given to the Levites and to the tribe of Judah, from which tribe the Davidic line is descended. The purpose of compiling these genealogies was to establish "the rights of the several Levitical families in post-exilic Jerusalem to fulfill their various functions . . . [and to support] the claim of other important families in the Jewish community to count themselves truly as children of Abraham, heirs of the divine promise."[5]

The Reign of David (I Chr. 10–29). Nearly all the material in the last twenty chapters of I Chronicles is taken from I and II Samuel and I Kings. The Chronicler begins with the death of Saul and ends with the death of David. In order to carry out his religio-ethical aims, he omits or changes many passages and adds a few of his own.

The most significant deletions are those concerning the conception, birth, and childhood of Samuel; the reign of Saul; David's slaying of Goliath; David's affair with Bathsheba; and Absalom's rebellion.

The principal additions made by the Chronicler are as follows: (1) attributing Saul's death to his consulting of the witch of Endor (10:13-14); (2) gathering of the armies at Hebron to proclaim David king of all Israel (12:23-40); (3) Hiram of Tyre's aid to David (14:1); (4) David's psalm of thanksgiving for the bringing of the Ark to Jerusalem (16:7-36); (5) David's contributions to the Temple (22:14-16 and 28:14-19);* (6) assignment of the Levites, singers, and other attendants in the Temple (23:2–27:34); (7) David's pattern for the Temple (28:11-13); and finally (8) David's last prayer (29:10-19).

The Reign of Solomon and the Subsequent History of Judah (II Chr.). The second book of Chronicles covers the reign of Solomon and the history of the kingdom of Judah from the reign

---

* Note that God forbade David to build the Temple "because thou has shed much blood upon the earth," and reserved that high privilege for David's peaceable son, Solomon, for whom God "will give peace and quietness unto Israel in his days." The Temple was to be the visible sign of God's presence, the symbol of Jerusalem as the holy city, and the center of the Hebrew faith.

of Rehoboam to the edict of Cyrus which permitted the Israelites to go back to Palestine. Thus the book repeats much of
I and II Kings. But it ignores the history of the kingdom of Israel except when the affairs of that kingdom are closely related
to those of Judah.

As in the case of I Chronicles, the author changes his sources
to suit his purposes. He whitewashes the character of Solomon,
saying nothing about his being led into idolatry by his multitude
of wives. He expands many passages which emphasize the work
of the prophets and their messages from God. For example, in I
Kings the account of the invasion of Palestine by Shishak is covered in four verses (14:25-28), whereas the Chronicler goes into
great detail about the invasion, the prophet Shemaiah's pro-
nouncements to Rehoboam, and that king's repentance—a total of
twelve verses (II Chr. 12:1-12). He stresses more the reigns of
four good kings of Judah—Asa, Jehoshaphat, Hezekiah, and
Josiah. He inserts two passages which enhance the prestige of
the Levites (20:19-21 and 31:2-19). He mentions by name the
prophet Jeremiah and tells of his predictions (36:21-22). And
finally, the Chronicler adds the passage telling of the Persian
conquest of Babylon and freeing of the exiles (36:20-23): "Thus
saith Cyrus king of Persia. All the kingdoms of the earth hath the
lord God of heaven given me; and he hath charged me to build
him an house in Jerusalem, which is in Judah. Who is there
among you of all his people? The Lord his God be with him,
and let him go up."

EZRA AND NEHEMIAH: THE CHRONICLER'S ACCOUNT OF THE REBUILDING OF JERUSALEM

In the ancient Jewish canon the books of Ezra and Nehemiah
formed a single work, entitled simply "Ezra." The division into
two parts was probably made in the Vulgate. The book of Ezra
derives its name from its main character, the priest who led religious reform in Jerusalem about 397 B.C. The book of Nehemiah
is named for its main character, the cupbearer of King Artaxerxes I or II.

One of the few matters concerning the books of Ezra and Nehemiah on which virtually all scholars agree is the fact that they
were written (or compiled) by the man responsible for the preparation of I and II Chronicles, the man known as "the Chron-

icler." In all four books he shows a fondness for lists, catalogues, and genealogies; an unusual interest in Temple procedures and the functions of the Levites; and what would seem today a lack of concern for chronological and historical accuracy. In the book of Ezra he skips without warning a period of several decades (after Ezra 6:22), and he shifts back and forth from first to third person, as if he is simply copying his sources verbatim. Some of the inaccuracies are attributable to the facts that the two books were probably written more than a century after the events described and that the events had occurred in a very unsettled period that left few reliable records.

For the book Ezra, the Chronicler *undoubtedly* used some official reports written in Aramaic * concerning the persecution of the Jews (Ezra 4:8–6:18 and 7:12-26); and he *probably* utilized (1) a memoir written by the priest Ezra,† (2) official Temple records, genealogies, and lists of names, and (3) oral traditions. The chief evidence in favor of his use of an account by Ezra himself is the fact that part of the narrative concerning that priest is written in the first person, whereas most of the book is in the third person.[6]

It should be noted here that the literary form known as the "epistle" (which was later to form a significant portion of the New Testament) makes its first appearance in the Holy Scriptures in Ezra. Four letters are included in the book: 4:11-16, 4:17-22, 5:7-17, and 7:12-26.

The principal source for the book of Nehemiah is a personal memoir written by Nehemiah himself (*c.* 432 B.C.). This memoir probably comprises Neh. 1:1–7:4, 11:1-2, 12:27-43, and 13:4-31,[7] sections which, taken together constitute a vital and intimate narrative revelatory of the personality and the religious devotion of its author. They are written in the first person.

---

* Aramaic is the language which resulted from the mingling of foreign elements with primitive Hebrew, especially during the Exile. By 300 B.C. Aramaic had almost entirely supplanted primitive Hebrew as the spoken language.

† Considering the Chronicler's tendency to idealize and invent, some reputable scholars have doubted the very existence of Ezra as a historical character and have believed him to be a figment of the Chronicler's imagination —an embodiment of priestly virtues as conceived by an ardent Levite. If Ezra never really existed, then it follows that the above-mentioned memoir by Ezra is spurious. This rather extreme view is not widely held today.

There is little doubt that a later copyist or redactor has disarranged the Ezra-Nehemiah narrative as written by the Chronicler, so that now it is decidedly chaotic. Parts of the Ezra narrative have been pulled out of the original account and transferred to Nehemiah.

In order to rearrange the passages correctly, we should have to solve another very difficult problem: did the man Ezra precede the man Nehemiah in point of time, or did he follow him? Ezra 6–9 says that the priest Ezra went to Jerusalem in the seventh year of the reign of Artaxerxes, and Neh. 2:1-5 says that in the twentieth year of Artaxerxes' reign Nehemiah requested permission to rebuild Jerusalem. Therefore many scholars have concluded that, since Artaxerxes I ruled 465-424 B.C., Ezra's reforms began in 458 and Nehemiah's journey to Jerusalem took place in 445 or 444. Other scholars, however, have argued rather convincingly that the activities of Nehemiah necessarily preceded Ezra's reforms; they point out, for example, that Nehemiah has to rebuild the wall of the city (Neh. 1:3) and that Ezra thanks God for the wall (Ezra 9:9); and that Nehemiah regrets that the number of Jews in Jerusalem is small (Neh. 7:4 and 11:1-2), whereas Ezra speaks of "a great congregation" (Ezra 10:1).[8] Therefore, these scholars believe, Ezra's monarch was Artaxerxes II, who reigned 404-358 B.C.; Ezra, then, would have gone to Jerusalem in 398 or 397 B.C. instead of in 458. It is pretty well established that Nehemiah's labors of reconstruction began in 444 B.C.

If Nehemiah's rebuilding of the city wall preceded Ezra's reforms, the material should be arranged as follows: Ezra 1–6, Neh. 1:1–7:4, Neh. 11-13, Ezra 7-8, Neh. 8, Ezra 9-10, and Neh. 7:5-73.[9] This arrangement seems the most logical one and for the purposes of the present Outline will be assumed.

Zerubbabel and the Temple (Ezra 1–6). The book of Ezra opens with a repetition of Cyrus' decree found at the end of II Chronicles. According to the Chronicler, Zerubbabel (or Sheshbazzar [10]) now gathers together a large number of Hebrews from the tribes of Benjamin and Judah and sets out for Jerusalem. They are allowed to take with them great quantities of the sacred vessels which Nebuchadrezzar had carried to Babylon. They set up a sacrificial altar, revive the observance of the Feast of Tabernacles (or Booths), and lay the foundations of a new Temple (536 B.C.).

Next the author records the beginning of the historic enmity between the Judeans and the Samaritans,* an enmity which lasted well past the time of Christ. The Samaritans, as worshipers of Yahweh, ask to be allowed to help in the building of the Temple. Zerubbabel refuses their aid, with the haughty remark that the Samaritans and the Jerusalem Jews have nothing in common. Thereafter the Samaritans successfully harass the restorers of the Temple till the second year of the reign of Darius I (520 B.C.).† Apparently it is these Samaritans, these "adversaries of Judah and Benjamin," who persuade Tatnai (Tattenai), the Persian governor of the province, to write to Darius about authority to rebuild the Temple. King Darius finds the old decree of Cyrus and issues a new one to the effect that the restorers are not to be hindered in their efforts. Four years later (516 B.C.) the Temple is completed and dedicated with great rejoicing.

Nehemiah's Petition (Neh. 1:1–2:8). About three generations after the reconstruction of the Temple, Nehemiah, the cupbearer of Artaxerxes I, records in his memoir the piteous condition of Jerusalem as reported to him in Susa (Shushan), the Persian capital, by some Hebrews who have just returned from Palestine: "The remnant that are left of the captivity there in the province are in great affliction and reproach; the wall of Jerusalem also is broken down, and the gates thereof are burned with fire." Nehemiah is so sorrowful that he sits down and weeps and for several days mourns and fasts and prays. Noticing his sad countenance, Artaxerxes asks the cause. "Then I was very sore afraid, and said unto the king, Let the king live for ever: why should not my countenance be sad, when the city, the place of my fathers' sepulchres, lieth waste, and the gates thereof are consumed with fire?" Artaxerxes inquires what he wants to do about

---

* The term *Samaritan* was applied not only to the inhabitants of the city of Samaria but also to all those who, after the fall of the kingdom of Israel, dwelt in the region around the Northern capital. For two reasons the Judean Hebrews looked with scorn upon the Samaritans: first, they considered the Samaritans to be "collaborationists" with the Assyrians and Babylonians; and second, they believed that the Samaritans had polluted the pure Hebrew blood by intermarriage with foreigners, a practice against which both Nehemiah and Ezra exhorted.

† Verses 5-23 of Ch. 4 are probably the Chronicler's addition to the narrative found in his sources. These verses refer to a later period (the reigns of Ahasuerus [Xerxes I], 486-465, and Artaxerxes I, 464-424) and tell about enemies who interrupted the building of the *walls*, not the Temple.

it. Again Nehemiah is afraid, but, after uttering a prayer to God, he begs to be allowed to go to Jerusalem and rebuild it. The king is gracious and, not in the least displeased, asks simply how long Nehemiah will be gone. He gives his cupbearer letters of recommendation and authority, and Nehemiah sets out.

Rebuilding of the Wall (Neh. 2:9—7:4). He arrives safely in the city, but his troubles are only beginning. His efforts are continually opposed by "foreigners," especially Sanballat the Horonite,* Tobiah the Ammonite, and Geshem the Arab. They accuse him of plotting to rebel against Artaxerxes and of wanting to make himself king. Nehemiah perseveres in spite of their accusations, and work on the wall begins. Sanballat and the others ridicule their efforts: "What do these feeble Jews? . . . will they revive the stones out of the heaps of the rubbish which are burned? . . . Even that which they build, if a fox go up, he shall even break down their stone wall." Five times Sanballat tries to lure Nehemiah away from the city so that he may harm or kill him, but Nehemiah will not be tricked. He steadfastly answers: . . . "I am doing a great work, so that I cannot come down: why should the work cease, whilst I leave it, and come down to you?" (Neh. 6:3). The enemies even threaten to make armed attacks on the builders of the wall, so that some of Nehemiah's men have to stop construction and stand guard. Every workman labors on the wall with one hand and carries a weapon in the other.

Nor are these the only difficulties which Nehemiah has to overcome. There is dissatisfaction among his own group. Many of them are suffering from economic distress. High taxes and famines have forced some to borrow from their more affluent Jewish brethren, who have been exacting exorbitant interest, foreclosing mortgages on property, and even enslaving the sons and daughters of those unable to pay their debts. Nehemiah rebukes the creditors, and work on rebuilding the wall continues.

After only fifty-two days the wall is completed and solemnly dedicated. Nehemiah sets appropriate guards about it and appoints priests and Levites to their various duties in the city.

Nehemiah's Reforms (Neh. 13). The former cupbearer's troubles are not yet over; he still has to solve many real problems—politi-

---

* Sanballat was apparently associated with the hostile Samaritans (see Neh. 4:2). A "Horonite" was an inhabitant of Beth-horon, a city of Ephraim.

cal, economic, religious, and social. While he is away on a visit to Susa, his priest Eliashib desecrates the Temple by allowing the pagan and alien Tobiah, Sanballat's crony, to live in a chamber of the building. Upon returning from Persia, Nehemiah casts Tobiah out and cleanses the Temple. Next, the Levites neglect their duties for the legitimate reason that they have not been paid their promised portions. Nehemiah conciliates them by collecting tithes and paying the overdue salaries. Then he discovers that the people are failing to keep the Sabbath day holy: they are allowing buying and selling to be carried on upon that day; he quickly puts a stop to this. Finally, one of Nehemiah's most serious problems is his people's intermarriage with foreigners—Ashdodites,* Ammonites, and Moabites. He is forced to use drastic measures: "And I contended with them, and cursed them, and smote certain of them, and plucked off their hair, and made them swear by God: Ye shall not give your daughters unto their sons, nor take their daughters for your sons, or for yourselves." These measures must have had some effect, for Nehemiah says that he has cleansed the Israelites from "strangers" (foreigners). The problem, however, is solved only temporarily; a few decades later Ezra is faced with it again.

Nehemiah ends his memoir with the characteristic prayer: "Remember me, O my God, for good" (Neh. 13:31).

Ezra's Reforms (Ezra 7–8; Neh. 8, Ezra 9–10; and Neh. 7:5-73). The second part of the book of Ezra opens with the introduction of Ezra himself, plus a tracing of his ancestry back to Aaron, the brother of Moses. (This genealogy is probably included to assure the reader that Ezra is of genuine priestly stock; the reader is also told that Ezra is a scribe learned in the law of Moses.) Ezra requests Artaxerxes to allow him to go to Jerusalem to teach Moses' law to the children of Israel there. Then follows a letter (in Aramaic) from Artaxerxes which not only grants Ezra's request but also allows him to take up a collection from the people in Babylon and to draw on the Persian treasury in each of the provinces through which he passes. Finally, the letter authorizes Ezra to appoint magistrates and to enforce laws.

Writing in the first person, Ezra bursts into an exuberant praise of God for putting such things into King Artaxerxes' heart.

---

* Ashdod was formerly a Philistine territory, and its people worshiped the god Dagon.

After proclaiming a fast, Ezra prepares to set out for Palestine. Here (still in the first person) he inserts a very interesting and very human comment. He says that he is making the journey without the protection of soldiers because he has told the king that God will be his protector; therefore he would have been ashamed to ask for a military convoy. Ezra and several companions make the journey in safety, deliver their treasures to the keepers of the Temple, and offer sacrifices to the Lord.

Now (Neh. 8:2) the people assemble. Ezra opens the book of Moses' law and reads to them.* The people weep, for they perceive how flagrantly they have been disobeying that law. Ezra comforts them.

Next, Ezra is greatly perturbed upon discovering that the Israelites of Jerusalem have been intermarrying with foreigners— Canaanites, Hittites, Perizzites, Jebusites, Ammonites, Moabites, Egyptians, and Amorites. Ezra tears his clothes, pulls out the hair of his head and beard, and sits down "astonied." The reasons for his grief are, first, that he does not want the Hebrew blood defiled, and second—and more important—that he fears the foreigners will lead the people of Israel away from the true God, as they had done in the days of Solomon and Ahab. Again he assembles the people and in their presence offers a prayer of confession to God. The people, too, confess their sins, promise to put away all alien spouses and their children, and never more to intermarry. A solemn feast of repentance is proclaimed, and after another prayer by the leader of the Levites, the people sign a covenant to abjure marriage with foreigners, to pay tithes, and to obey the law of the Lord.

Thus the account of Ezra's reforms ends on a happy note.

I ESDRAS: A SECOND POST-EXILIC ACCOUNT OF JEWISH HISTORY FROM JOSIAH TO THE REBUILDING OF JERUSALEM

The word *Esdras* is the Greek form of *Ezra*. In Protestant Bibles the book is known as "I Esdras" and is part of the Apocrypha; in Roman Catholic (Douay) Bibles it is a canonical book and is called "III Esdras" (I and II Esdras in Catholic Bibles are, respectively, Ezra and Nehemiah in Protestant Scriptures).

---

* An interesting linguistic fact is here preserved. The people no longer understand pure Hebrew, and Ezra has to use interpreters to explain his reading to the people. See Neh. 8:7-8.

Modern scholars believe that I Esdras is a fragment of a Greek translation (*c.* 150 B.C.) of the work of the Chronicler—Chronicles and Ezra-Nehemiah—a translation older than the canonical version preserved in the Septuagint. The translator responsible for I Esdras was probably an Alexandrian Jew.[11]

This Apocryphal book is a freer and more idiomatic translation of the Chronicler's narrative than the canonical one. It covers the period from the last days of Josiah to Ezra's reading of the law to the people of Jerusalem.

Significant Departures from the Ezra-Nehemiah Account. There are two significant differences between the account of the rebuilding of Jerusalem as given in I Esdras and that given in the books of Ezra and Nehemiah. In the first place, I Esdras 2 says that Artaxerxes orders the rebuilding of Jerusalem and its Temple to cease, because the Samaritans have written him a letter warning that the Jews are planning a rebellion; this account says that the work of reconstruction ceased till the second year of the reign of Darius.* In the second place, I Esdras makes no mention at all of Nehemiah.

The Contest of the Three Guardsmen (3–4). An interesting addition to the old story of Zerubbabel has some of the characteristics of a folk tale, a medieval *débat,* and even a Platonic dialogue.[12] Zerubbabel (Zorobabel) is one of the three bodyguards of King Darius.† These young men suggest a contest to be held before the king. Each of them is to nominate the strongest thing in the world and then to defend his nomination; the king and his noblemen are to be the judges of the wisdom of the three speeches and to choose the winner. The three bodyguards also suggest that the winner be given an appropriate prize. Darius approves the contest.

The first guardsman says that *wine* is the strongest of all things, because it can make a man sinful, happy, belligerent, or self-confident. The second guardsman argues that the *king* is the strongest, for he can impose his will on all others. But Zerubbabel wins, first, by demonstrating in great detail that *woman* is able to bend any man (even a king) to her will, and, second, by pointing out that *truth* is stronger even than woman, because it endures forever, is approved by all, and is an attribute of God.

---

* Contrast the account found in Ezra 5:3–6:22.

† In the book of Ezra, Zerubbabel is a subject of Cyrus, not of Darius.

The court, of course, cheers the speech of Zerubbabel and adjudges him the wisest, and his wisdom finds favor in the sight of Darius. Instead of choosing gold or other riches, Zerubbabel asks that Darius permit him to take back to Jerusalem the vessels which have been carried away by Nebuchadrezzar and to rebuild the Temple. Darius kisses him and grants his request.

Thus does I Esdras provide an explanation for Darius' kindness to the Jews.

6

The Maccabean Revolt

I and II Maccabees

There is no Biblical record of the events which took place in Palestine between the time of Ezra's reforms (c. 397 B.C.) and the early part of the second century B.C. During that long period, however, many things happened which affected the future of the Hebrews. In 331 B.C. the Persian empire fell before the onslaughts of Alexander the Great, who had conquered Palestine in 332 B.C., and he soon took over the rule of all Persian-held territories. When Alexander died in 323 B.C., his empire was divided among four of his generals. The eastern, or Syrian, section became the portion of Seleucus and his descendants, known as the Seleucids. The southern, or Egyptian, area (which included Palestine) fell to Ptolemy * and his descendants; under these monarchs the Hebrews enjoyed a mild and tolerant rule similar to that which they had enjoyed under the Persians; they had virtually complete religious freedom and a considerable degree of autonomy. Then in 198 B.C., Antiochus III, the Seleucid king of Syria, defeated the Egyptians near Mount Hermon and made Palestine part of his kingdom. The policy of the Seleucids, very different from that of the Ptolemies, was to impose Greek customs, language, and religion upon all the people in their dominions. Abhorrent as this policy was to many of the Hebrews, there was no open rebellion until Antiochus IV (Epiphanes) in 168 B.C. erected an altar to the Greek god Zeus in the Temple at Jerusalem. The uprising which ensued in 167 B.C.—led by Judas Maccabeus and other members of his family—continued more than thirty years

---

* Ptolemy II (Philadelphus), who ruled c. 285-c. 246 B.C. is traditionally reputed to have sponsored the preparation of the Septuagint.

and at last succeeded in giving the Jewish people a large measure of political and religious freedom and a dynasty of Hebrew rulers for almost a century.

The following table [1] outlines the most significant events of the Maccabean period:

198 B.C.	Antiochus III, the Seleucid king of Syria, defeats Egypt, annexes Palestine, and tries to Hellenize the Hebrews.
175 B.C.	Antiochus IV (Epiphanes) accedes to throne, continues Hellenization of Palestine. "Collaborationist" Hebrews build gymnasium for Greek type of athletics in Jerusalem.
171 B.C.	Antiochus IV sacks Temple in Jerusalem.
168 B.C.	Antiochus IV perpetrates many atrocities against the Hebrews in Jerusalem. In 167 B.C. the priest Mattathias, of the Hasmon family,* leads some Hebrews in revolt. Several battles follow.
166 B.C.	Mattathias dies and is succeeded as military leader by his son Judas Maccabeus, who wins several victories over the Syrians.
165 B.C.	Judas purifies Temple, inaugurates Hebrew festival of Hanukkah.
161 B.C.	Judas defeats Syrians under General Nicanor, inaugurates Jewish festival of Nicanor's Day. Judas makes mutual-assistance pact with Rome.
160 B.C.	Judas slain in battle, succeeded as military leader of Hebrews by his brother Jonathan. War continues two more years.
158-153 B.C.	Peace with the Syrians.
142 B.C.	Jonathan slain by enemy, is succeeded by his brother Simon, who continues war, defeats Syrians, wins virtual independence for the Jews. Peace for seven years.
134 B.C.	War resumed. Simon slain by his own son-in-law; succeeded as priest-king by his son John Hyrcanus.
134-104 B.C.	Reign of John Hyrcanus, marked by peace and prosperity. Rise of Pharisees and Sadducees.
104-63 B.C.	Period of internal unrest and civil wars.
63 B.C.	Pompey the Great called in to settle dispute over throne, establishes Roman control over Palestine; Hasmoneans are puppet-kings.

* Mattathias' descendants are known as the Hasmonaeans, as well as Maccabees.

40 B.C.   Herod the Great appointed King of Judea, replacing
                 the Hasmonaean dynasty.

The Maccabean period witnessed the rise of two religio-politi-
cal parties which were later to be of great importance: the Sadducees and the Pharisees. Though not even mentioned in the
canonical books of the Old Testament, in the New Testament
they are treated as long-established and influential sects.

The Sadducees were "the aristocratic supporters of the Maccabean dynasty, the wealthy minority from which the priesthood
was recruited." [2] Generally they rejected belief in personal immortality and looked with distrust upon anything miraculous or
apocalyptic. "Educated, worldly and more than tinged with
Hellenism, they wished to confine their religion to what was
literally 'written in the law of Moses' and rejected the traditional rules and ceremonies, taught by the Pharisees, not literally
supported by Biblical authority." [3]

Opposed to the Sadducees were the Pharisees, usually identified with the Hasidim (or Assideans). In I Maccabees 2:42 the
Hasidim are described as mighty warriors. In later times the
Pharisees were recognized as a pious group of teachers who
stressed not only the Mosaic law but also the traditional priestly
or rabbinical interpretations of that law which had been handed
down since the time of Ezra. The term *Pharisee* (an Aramaic word
meaning "the separated") was first applied to a member of this
group about 110 to 105 B.C. and apparently referred to "their
meticulous care in avoiding anything ceremonially unclean." [4] By
the time of Christ the rabbinical interpretations of the law had
become excessively numerous and complicated, and Christ on
some occasions attacked the Pharisees, apparently because he felt
that many of them were more interested in the letter of the law
than in its spirit or in genuine goodness. Although *Pharisaism*
is today almost synonymous with hypocritical self-righteousness,
in the first century A.D. and earlier, to be a Pharisee was an honor.
St. Paul was brought up as one (see Acts 23:6), and some scholars
have claimed that Christ himself was a Pharisee.

It was in Maccabean times, too, that belief in personal immortality came to be widespread. In most Old Testament books
written before the second century B.C., little is said about the
afterlife. Sheol, it is true, is frequently mentioned, but it is always

a shadowy underground place where, upon dying, men are "gathered" to their people; it is a region neither of punishment for the wicked nor of reward for the righteous.* So far as is known, the eighth-century prophet Isaiah was the first Biblical writer to mention bodily resurrection (Isa. 26:19). Many generations, however, were to pass before belief in the "resurrection of the body and the life everlasting"—one of the central tenets of Christian theology—became an important part of Hebrew doctrine. The best pre-Christian statement of this belief appears in II Maccabees.

It is worth noting here that the epistle, which had already appeared as a literary type in the book of Ezra (see above, p. 136), plays an important role in the two books of Maccabees. Six letters appear in I Maccabees (8:23-27, 31:32; 10:18-20, 52-54; 13:36-40; and 15:2-9) and two in II Maccabees (1:1-9 and 1:10—2:18).

The two books of Maccabees are named for Judas Maccabeus, one of the great Hebrew military heroes whose deeds are narrated in these books. The word *Maccabeus* probably means "hammer" or "hammerer."[5]

I MACCABEES: HISTORY OF THE REVOLT
FROM 168 TO 135 B.C.

The name of the author of I Maccabees is unknown. Some scholars believe him to have been a Sadducee, but evidence that he was is inconclusive.[6] The book was first written in Hebrew at some time between 135 and 63 B.C., probably shortly after 100 B.C.[7]

All commentators agree that the book is, in the main, a trustworthy historical narrative. It is especially accurate and valuable as a record of dates; each event is dated according to the year of the reign of the Seleucids, who began their rule in late 312 or early 311 B.C.[8] Although strongly partisan in favor of the Maccabees, the author gives an almost completely unprejudiced report, telling the failures as well as the successes of his protagonists. He has little or nothing to say about miracles or supernatural happenings. His style is plain, rapid, and straightforward; he gives few details about the battles he records.

Although he does not have so didactic an intent as either the author of Kings or the "Chronicler," it may be said that his his-

* See, for example, Gen. 25:8, 35:29, 49:29, and Deut. 32:50.

tory illustrates the thesis that the faithful and courageous will gain success and glory.[9]

After a brief introduction summarizing the period from Alexander's conquest of Persia down to Antiochus III's defeat of Egypt, the author launches into his main task of telling about Antiochus Epiphanes' attempts to wipe out the Judaistic religion, the resultant rebellion, and the establishment of the Maccabean (or Hasmonaean) dynasty, which was to last till 40 B.C. The book covers the period 168-135 B.C. In addition to the main narrative thread, which is concerned with the Jewish resistance to Syrian oppression, the book contains many records of international politics, intrigues, treaties, abrogations of treaties, and treachery; these records are too numerous and too confusing (without extensive explanatory notes) to be treated here, but they are of great value to students of ancient Oriental history.

The Atrocities of Antiochus Epiphanes (Ch. 1). After a victorious expedition against Egypt, in 168 B.C. Antiochus Epiphanes decides to enforce upon Jerusalem his policy of Hellenization. He robs the Temple of its golden altar, its candlestick, and its gold and silver vessels. Somewhat later he sends to the city his tribute collector, who kills many of the people, takes many others captive, sets fire to the buildings, and pulls down the houses and the walls. Next Antiochus builds a great citadel in Jerusalem and puts into it a garrison of Syrian soldiers. Worst of all, as far as the faithful worshipers of Yahweh are concerned, he sends a decree over his whole kingdom that everybody is to follow the Greek religion. He burns copies of the Mosaic law and forbids the offering of sacrifices to any but Greek gods, the circumcision of children, and the observance of the Sabbath and festival days. Antiochus' men hang circumcised infants about their mothers' necks and then kill these mothers. Perhaps the last straw is the building of an altar to Zeus in Yahweh's own Temple and the sacrificing there of swine, an abomination to devout Jews. The historian sadly admits that many Jews give in to Antiochus' demands and embrace the pagan religion which he advocates; but many others eschew the pagan ceremonies, choosing to die rather than to profane the holy covenant.

Mattathias (Ch. 2). One of those who refuse to obey the orders of the king is the priest Mattathias. He and his five sons—Joannan, Simon, Judas, Eleazar, and Jonathan—move away from Jeru-

salem; they mourn for the city and its people, and they continue
to worship the true God.* When Mattathias sees a Hebrew offering a sacrifice on a heathen altar, he slays the man forthwith. He
also kills the king's commissioner, pulls down the altar, and then
flees with his sons to the mountains. Other faithful Hebrews join
them.

A sad but interesting story is told concerning a thousand of the
most pious refugees who refuse to offer resistance to the Syrians
on the Sabbath and so are slaughtered. Mattathias and his im-
mediate friends, however, decide that self-defense is justifiable,
even on the Sabbath.

Eventually Mattathias and his group are strong enough to
carry on guerrilla warfare against the Syrians. They destroy many
heathen altars and forcibly circumcise many Hebrew children.

When Mattathias feels that his life is drawing to a close, he
appoints Judas Maccabeus, the mightiest of his sons, to be military commander.

Judas Maccabeus (3–9:22). Judas now assumes leadership of
the rebels in their struggle for religious freedom. He is a superb
leader, as a poem (3:2-9) indicates: "In his acts . . . like a lion,
and like a lion's whelp, roaring for his prey." In addition to being
a shrewd and valiant soldier, he is also an eloquent orator. Before
each battle he exhorts his men to remember how God has helped
the Hebrews in times past, and he assures them that God will
still be their protector. With fasting and prayer they prepare for
battle, placing their trust in God.

The Syrians now oppose the Hebrews in force. Despite over-
whelming odds, Judas and his men defeat Antiochus' armies in
several major battles. During the course of one of these encounters, the Syrians employ elephants against Judas' men—the first
military use of elephants in recorded history (6:30). Judas'
brother Eleazar, believing the Syrian king to be upon one particular elephant, valiantly attacks the beast and kills it by striking
it on the underside. The elephant falls upon Eleazar and kills
him.

After a number of decisive victories, Judas is able to march
into Jerusalem, cleanse the Temple, and build a new altar. For
eight days the Hebrew people offer sacrifices to God and cele-

---

* Three of these sons—Simon, Judas, and Jonathan—are to play important
roles in the history of the period.

brate the dedication of the new altar "with mirth and gladness." Thus Judas inaugurates the great festival known as Hanukkah (or Chanukah), which is still observed today (4:36-59).

Soon after the death of Antiochus Epiphanes (*c.* 164 B.C.), Judas makes peace with the Syrians and succeeds in winning religious freedom for his people—the main objective for which he has been striving (6:60).

Three years later war breaks out again, and once more Judas is victorious. He defeats the Syrian general Nicanor and celebrates his victory by inaugurating the festival known as Nicanor's Day, observed annually for more than two centuries (7:49).[10]

Next Judas makes a mutual-assistance pact with Rome (Ch. 8). This is of great significance, for it is the Hebrews' first official dealing with the great new empire of the West (161 B.C.).

The following year Judas is slain in battle (9:1-27).

Jonathan Apphus (9:28—12). Judas Maccabeus is succeeded by his brother Jonathan as military leader of the Jews. With the aid of Simon, another son of Mattathias, Jonathan rallies the Jewish forces and defeats the Syrians. After a two-year peace the Syrians try another battle but are once more defeated (158 B.C.). Now they agree to a covenant with the Hebrews, and the latter enjoy a five-year period of peace (9:70-73). Jonathan is appointed by the Syrian ruler to be high priest of Israel; this appointment is a very important event, inasmuch as the priesthood thenceforth becomes hereditary. Thus is established the line of priest-kings which is to rule the Israelites till 40 B.C.

During the period of Jonathan's leadership of the Jews, Syria suffers from much internal political intrigue and civil war. Once when Jonathan sides with one Syrian faction, another lures him into a Syrian city with a declaration of friendship, treacherously takes Jonathan prisoner, and slays all his men (142 B.C.).

Simon Thassi (Chs. 13—16). Now it is Simon's turn to exhort the Hebrews to oppose the tyranny which threatens them. He gathers an army and marches against the enemy faction of the Syrians; the leader of the faction tries to deceive him by promising to free Jonathan on condition that Simon will send him two hundred talents of silver plus Jonathan's two sons. Simon is not deceived, but sends the sons and the silver lest the Hebrew people accuse him of not trying to save Jonathan. The Syrians kill Jonathan anyhow and retreat.

Judea enjoys peace for about seven years. Simon strengthens his position by building fortresses all over the land and putting garrisons into them. He also forms an alliance with the Syrian king, who confirms his appointment as high priest and who releases the Israelites from the payment of all taxes and tributes. Thus Simon succeeds in winning for his people virtually complete political independence (142 B.C.).

In 134 B.C. the Syrians begin once more to persecute the Hebrews and to slay them, so that the followers of Simon have to defend themselves again. Simon being very old, his two sons, Judas and John, lead the people against the Syrians and win a victory. Simon and his sons Mattathias and Judas are treacherously slain by Simon's own son-in-law. John (surnamed Hyrcanus) succeeds his father as priest-king (134 B.C.).

Thus ends the history of the Jews insofar as it is to be found in the Apocrypha.

II MACCABEES: A PHARISAIC VIEW OF THE REVOLT
FROM C. 176 TO 161 B.C.

The second book of Maccabees is not, as one might expect, a sequel to I Maccabees. Instead it is a retelling of approximately the first seven chapters of that history, and it covers a period of about fifteen years as opposed to the thirty-three years of I Maccabees.

This anonymous book is believed to have been written in Greek by a pious Alexandrian Hebrew of strong Pharisaic tendencies. It purports to be a condensation of a five-volume work by one Jason of Cyrene. Whereas the author of I Maccabees may have showed Sadducean leanings, the author of II Maccabees emphasizes the belief in immortality, miracles, the supernatural, and the apocalyptic. The date of composition is uncertain. Scholars have suggested various times, ranging from 125 B.C. to about a century later.[11]

As a record of events, it is far less trustworthy than I Maccabees. It "reads more like religious pleading than history or literature. . . ."[12] Its aim is to teach religious truths as conceived by the Pharisees of the second (or first) century B.C.

The style of II Maccabees is more rhetorical, more florid, less rapid, and less concise than that of I Maccabees.

The book opens with two prefatory letters (1:1-9 and 1:10–2:18)—both written by the Hebrews in Judea and addressed to the Hebrews in Egypt and both telling of some of the hardships suffered by the Judean Hebrews. Chapters 3–5 give an account of how the Maccabean revolt broke out; chapters 6–7 give more details about the persecution of the Hebrews; and chapters 8–15 cover the revolt up to Nicanor's Day.

The details of some incidents—especially of miracles—and some theological doctrines as covered in II Maccabees are worthy of special notice.

The Vision of Heliodorus (Ch. 3). Apparently during the reign of Antiochus III,* Onias, priest of the Temple in Jerusalem, becomes involved in an argument with Simon, governor of the Temple, over the matter of "disorder in the city." Spitefully Simon informs the king that the treasury of the Temple holds "infinite sums of money." The king sends his treasurer, Heliodorus, to Jerusalem to fetch the money. When he arrives, Onias informs him that Simon has exaggerated—that the Temple has only four hundred talents of silver and two hundred talents of gold. Furthermore, Onias says, that is laid by for the relief of widows and fatherless children. Regardless, Heliodorus prepares to take money. Onias is nearly prostrate with grief: "Then whoso had looked the high priest in the face, it would have wounded his heart; for his countenance and the changing of his colour declared the inward agony of his mind." The people join him in demonstrations of grief, and Onias begs God to save the treasury. As Heliodorus and his men come to take the money, God causes a miracle. A terrible warrior, clad in gold armor and seated upon a horse, appears before Heliodorus. The horse smites Heliodorus with its forefeet, so that the man is "compassed with great darkeness" and has to be borne off on a litter. Lest the king think that his treasurer has simply been attacked by the Jews, Onias prays God to spare Heliodorus' life. The prayer is granted, and Heliodorus offers thanks and a sacrifice to the Lord. When he returns to the king, he tells that monarch that "he that dwelleth in

* The historian is vague about this date, but a later reference (4:1-10) to the death of "the king" and the accession of Antiochus Epiphanes leads one to believe that the events related in Chapter 3 occurred during the reign of Antiochus III.

heaven hath his eye on that place and defendeth it, and he beat-
eth and destroyeth them that come to hurt it."

Onias and Jason (4:1–5:27). Onias has a wicked brother Jason,
who is a Greek sympathizer. Jason "labors underhand" to supplant Onias as high priest; he promises Antiochus Epiphanes
three hundred sixty talents of silver, plus a revenue of eighty
more, if the king will appoint him high priest in Onias' stead. He
also offers Antiochus a hundred fifty talents for a license to build
a gymnasium "for training up of youth in the fashions of the
heathen." The king accepts Jason's money, and Jason undertakes
a thorough Hellenization of his fellow Hebrews. Two years later,
however, Jason is superseded as high priest by Menelaus, who
promises the king five hundred sixty talents of silver; Jason is
forced to flee to the land of the Ammonites. Menelaus is even
worse than Jason, "bringing nothing worthy the high priesthood,
but having the fury of a cruel tyrant and the rage of a savage
beast." He robs the Temple treasury to pay his debt to the king.
Now, hearing the rumor that Antiochus has been killed in battle
in Egypt, Jason raises some troops and attacks Menelaus. The report of Antiochus' death proving false, Menelaus flees to the king
for protection. Antiochus returns from Egypt, reinstates Menelaus,
and punishes Jerusalem by raiding the Temple and slaughtering the people. This is the raid which leads to the Maccabean
rebellion.

The Courage of Eleazar the Scribe (Ch. 6). During the course
of Antiochus' persecution of Jerusalem, one Eleazar, an aged
scribe, is ordered by the king's men to eat some swine's flesh. He
is forced to put some of the pork into his mouth but, "choosing
rather to die gloriously than to live stained with such an abomination," spits it out. Then those "in charge of the wicked feast,"
taking pity on the old man, tell him that he may bring his own
meat and *pretend* that he is eating flesh of the swine. After thinking over the proposal, he declines and wills them "straightway to
send him to the grave," for, he says, "many young persons might
think that Eleazar, being fourscore years old and ten, were now
gone to a strange religion; and so they through mine hypocrisy
and desire to live a little time and a moment longer, should be
deceived by me, and I get a stain on mine old age and make it
abominable." Thereupon he is flogged to death, but he leaves "his

death for an example of a noble courage and a memorial of virtue, not only unto young men but unto all his nation."

The Massacre of the Seven Brothers (Ch. 7). Now seven young men and their mother are ordered to eat swine's flesh; when they refuse, they are "tormented with scourges and whips." Resolutely one of them tells their tormentors that they had rather die than transgress the laws of their fathers. This reply so enrages the king that he orders pans and caldrons to be heated, and he commands his men to seize the brother who has spoken so bravely, to cut out his tongue, to cut off the "utmost" parts of his body, and to fry him in a pan while the remainder of his family watches. One by one each brother is tortured in this manner, but each one exhorts the others not to weaken, and each dies professing faith in God and a belief that he will be raised up "unto everlasting life." The mother, too, is equally brave and equally resolute. She is massacred last of the eight.

Judas' Prayer and Offering for the Souls of the Dead (12:36-45). Judas Maccabeus prepares to bury some of his soldiers who have been slain in battle. He and his men discover under the coats of the slain "things consecrated to the idols of the Jamnites, which is forbidden the Jews by law." Then, says the historian, every man attributes the death of each of these soldiers to the sinful dependence on heathen talismans; and Judas' men pray God that their deceased fellows' sins "might wholly be put out of remembrance." Furthermore Judas takes up an offering and sends it to Jerusalem "to offer a sin offering, doing therein very well and honestly, in that he was mindful of the resurrection: for if he had not hoped that they that were slain should have risen again, it had been superfluous and vain to pray for the dead."

This passage is of special significance for two reasons. In the first place, belief in the resurrection of the dead (a tenet that is fundamental among Christians) is a Pharisaic belief, as was mentioned above; the Sadducees did not adhere to this doctrine. In the second place, the passage is partially responsible for the Protestant rejection of II Maccabees as a canonical book. Most Protestant sects strongly disapprove of prayers for the dead and of offering money to redeem a soul from punishment in the afterlife.

Judas' Vision of Onias (15:1-16). Directly before the great battle against Nicanor's army, Judas Maccabeus delivers a rousing oration to his men. In the course of his exhortations, he tells them that he has just had a dream, in which there appeared the figure of the dead Onias, holding up his hands and praying for the whole body of the Hebrew people.

This done, in like manner there appeared a man with gray hairs, and exceeding glorious, who was of a wonderful and excellent majesty. Then Onias answered, saying, "This is a lover of the brethren, who prayeth much for the people, and for the holy city, to wit, Jeremias the prophet of God." Whereupon Jeremias holding forth his right hand gave to Judas a sword of gold, and in giving it spake thus, "Take this holy sword, a gift from God, with which thou shalt wound the adversaries."

After Judas' speech the men are filled with confidence.

Then Nicanor and they that were with him came forward with trumpets and songs. But Judas and his company encountered the enemies with invocation and prayer. So that fighting with their hands, and praying unto God with their hearts, they slew no less than thirty and five thousand men; for through the appearance of God they were greatly cheered.

Nicanor is one of the slain, and Judas has Nicanor's head severed from his body. He cuts out the tongue and has his men "give it by pieces to the fowls," and he hangs the head on a tower as a "manifest sign unto all of the help of the Lord." Then Judas inaugurates the great festival of Nicanor's Day.

At this point the author concludes his tale with an engaging passage—a passage which is eminently appropriate for the ending of the history of the Jews before the time of Christ:

And here will I make an end. And if I have done well, and as is fitting the story, it is that which I desired: but if slenderly and meanly, it is that which I could attain to. For as it is hurtful to drink wine or water alone; and as wine mingled with water is pleasant, and delighteth the taste; even so speech finely framed delighteth the ears of them that read the story. And here shall be an end.

Notes

NOTES TO CHAPTER 1: PALESTINE AND ITS PEOPLE

[1] See W. F. Albright in *The Old Testament and Modern Study*, ed. H. H. Rowley. (London: Oxford University Press, 1951) pp. 6 ff. Oxford paperback edition, 1961.

[2] George Sprau, *Literature in the Bible* (New York: Macmillan Co., 1932), p. 41, doubts that all the tribes left Palestine and suggests that the whole account of the Egyptian residence may have been merely a symbolic representation of Egyptian supremacy over Palestine. Edgar J. Goodspeed, *How to Read the Bible* (Philadelphia: John C. Winston Co., 1946), p. 212, seems to accept the Biblical account literally when he says: "The Hebrews, enslaved and overworked in Egypt by Rameses II, in the thirteenth century before Christ, escaped from the country toward 1200 B.C." A number of scholars interpret pre-Mosaic accounts as symbology or as tribal rather than personal history. See Theodore H. Robinson, *The Interpreter's Bible* (Nashville, Tenn.: Abingdon Press, 1952), I, 273.

[3] For the date and identity of Moses' Pharaoh, see W. F. Albright, *op. cit.*, pp. 9-11; see also Chapter 3, note 13.

[4] William F. Albright, "The Old Testament World," *The Interpreter's Bible*, I, 235-236.

[5] For a detailed discussion of Hebrew faith and conception of God, see James Muilenburg, "The History of the Religion of Israel," *The Interpreter's Bible*, I, 292-389.

NOTES TO CHAPTER 2: THE NATURE, ORIGINS, AND CONTENTS OF THE BIBLE

[1] I am indebted for this point to J. H. Gardiner, *The Bible as English Literature* (New York: Charles Scribner's Sons, 1927), p. 1. Pages 1-12 of this book argue eloquently for the unity of the Bible.

[2] Stanley Rypins, *The Book of Thirty Centuries* (New York: Macmillan Co., 1951), p. 22.

[3] Rypins, *op. cit.* p. 310.

[4] Allen P. Wikgren, "The English Bible," *The Interpreter's Bible* (Nashville, Tenn.: Abingdon Press, 1952), I, 91. See also F. F. Bruce, *The English Bible* (New York: Oxford University Press, 1961), pp. 86-92.

[5] Wikgren, *The Interpreter's Bible*, I, 91.

[6] Wikgren, *The Interpreter's Bible*, I, 93.

[7] For the best discussion of what the King James Version owes to each of its English predecessors, see Charles C. Butterworth, *The Literary Lineage of the King James Bible, 1340-1611* (Philadelphia: University of Pennsylvania Press, 1941), p. 111.

[8] Wikgren, *The Interpreter's Bible*, I, 94-95.

[9] *The Holy Bible*, ed. John P. O'Connell (Chicago: The Catholic Press, 1950), p. x. For a list of revisions of Catholic Bibles, see Wikgren, *The Interpreter's Bible*, I, 100.

[10] Ira Maurice Price, *The Ancestry of Our English Bible*, ed. William A. Irwin and Allen P. Wikgren (3rd rev. ed.; New York: Harper & Brothers, 1956), p. 297.

[11] Price, *op. cit.*, p. 297.

[12] See Wikgren, *The Interpreter's Bible*, I, 99, for a brief summary. For a far longer account, see Max L. Margolis, *The Story of Bible Translations* (Philadelphia: Jewish Publication Society, 1917).

[13] See *The Holy Scriptures* (Philadelphia: Jewish Publication Society, 1917), preface, pp. vi-vii.

[14] Quoted by Price *op. cit.* p. 310.

NOTES TO CHAPTER 3:
THE FOUNDING OF THE HEBREW NATION

[1] See Cuthbert A. Simpson, "The Growth of the Hexateuch," *The Interpreter's Bible* (Nashville, Tenn.: Abingdon Press, 1952), I, 185, for a discussion of the traditional authorship of the Pentateuch.

[2] For an exciting account of the growth of the Hexateuch, see Simpson, *The Interpreter's Bible*, I, 185-200. This Outline is indebted to Simpson's account for much material on this topic.

[3] For the date of the J Document and its two editions (J^1 and J^2), see Simpson, *The Interpreter's Bible*, I, 192-196; and Harold H. Watts, *The Modern Reader's Guide to the Bible* (rev. ed.; New York: Harper & Brothers, 1959), p. 55.

[4] See Simpson, *The Interpreter's Bible*, I, 194, 200.

[5] William Owen Sypherd, *The Literature of the English Bible* (New York: Oxford University Press, 1938), p. 54. For a more nearly complete list of J passages, see Julius A. Bewer, *The Literature of the Old Testament* (rev. by Emil G. Kraeling; New York: Columbia University Press, 1962), footnotes to pp. 69-71.

⁶ For the date of the E Document, see Simpson, *The Interpreter's Bible*, I, 197, 200; and Watts, *op. cit.*, p. 55. Bewer, *op. cit.*, p. 85, and Alice Parmelee, *A Guidebook to the Bible* (New York: Harper & Brothers, 1948), p. 33, suggest 750 B.C. as a more likely date.

⁷ Sypherd, *op. cit.*, p. 54. For a more nearly complete list, see Bewer, *op. cit.*, pp. 79-88, *passim*, and especially footnotes to pp. 82, 83, and 84.

⁸ For a discussion of the virtual identity of Josiah's book of law and our Deuteronomy, see Simpson, *The Interpreter's Bible*, I, 197-198.

⁹ For a list of passages from the P Document, see Bewer, *op. cit.*, footnotes to pp. 260-264.

¹⁰ Edgar J. Goodspeed and J. M. Powis Smith (eds.), *The Short Bible* (Chicago: University of Chicago Press, 1933), p. 148.

¹¹ Theodore, H. Robinson, "The History of Israel," *The Interpreter's Bible*, I, 273. For a slightly different chronology of early Biblical events, see Watts, *op. cit.*, p. 70; and George A. Barrois, "Chronology, Metrology, etc.," *The Interpreter's Bible*, I, 142-152.

¹² Circumcision was also widely practiced by other Semites and by the Egyptians. See Cuthbert A. Simpson, Exegesis to Genesis, *The Interpreter's Bible*, I, 613-614.

¹³ For the identity of the oppressor and for that of the Pharoah of the Exodus, see Robinson, *The Interpreter's Bible*, I, 274; see also the discussion and bibliography given by J. Coert Rylaarsdam, Introduction to Exodus, *The Interpreter's Bible*, I, 836. Rameses II (*c.* 1290-1224 B.C.) is usually recognized as the oppressor; Seti I (1319-1301) and Tutmose III (*c.* 1450) have also been suggested.

¹⁴ An interesting analogue is the birth story of Sargon of Agade. See Rylaarsdam, Exegesis to Exodus, *The Interpreter's Bible*, I, 859. For a list of other "mysterious birth" stories, see Sypherd, *op. cit.*, p. 58. One should also note the parallel of the birth and saving of Jesus after the decree of Herod (Matt. 2).

¹⁵ The Egyptian form of the name seems to have been *Mes*. The Hebrew was *Môsheh*, from *māsāh*, meaning "to draw out." Perhaps this refers to Moses' drawing his people out of Egypt, or maybe to Pharaoh's daughter drawing Moses out of the water. See Rylaarsdam, Exegesis, *The Interpreter's Bible*, I, 861.

¹⁶ Mary Ellen Chase, *The Bible and the Common Reader* (rev. ed.; New York: Macmillan Co., 1952), p. 98.

¹⁷ For other explanations of the rite of Unleavened Bread, see Rylaarsdam, Exegesis, *The Interpreter's Bible*, I, 922.

¹⁸ Scholars believe that perhaps only the portions of the lyric in 15:1 should be attributed to Moses. (This is a quotation from the Song of Miriam, Ex. 15:20-22.) The following seventeen verses were probably added many centuries later.

[19] Apparently *Sinai* and *Horeb* are two names for the same mountain. Documents J and P use *Sinai*; E and D use *Horeb*. Some scholars think that there are two mountains referred to. For discussions of this question and of the identity of the mountain, see Rylaarsdam, Introduction, *The Interpreter's Bible*, I, 836-837.

[20] Ernest Wright, Exegesis to Deuteronomy, *The Interpreter's Bible* (Nashville, Tenn.: Abingdon Press, 1953), II, 454.

[21] Rylaarsdam, Exegesis, *The Interpreter's Bible*, I, 1042.

[22] Rylaarsdam, Introduction, *The Interpreter's Bible*, I, 842-843.

[23] *New Analytical Indexed* Bible (Chicago: John A. Dickson Co., 1931), p. 120.

[24] The Ark was probably originally a mere box. Later on in Hebrew history the Ark was of immense significance as the abode of God himself. It was sometimes carried into battle and even captured by the enemy (see I Sam. 4:11). Such a palladium was often carried about by nomadic tribes. See Rylaarsdam, *The Interpreter's Bible*, I, Introduction and Exegesis, 844-845 and 1022.

[25] The Tabernacle as described in Exodus would be far from a portable structure, but the description is anachronistic, being an idealized conception of the Tabernacle based on later writers' knowledge of the Temple in Jerusalem. See Rylaarsdam, Introduction, *The Interpreter's Bible*, I, 845.

[26] Roy B. Chamberlin and Herman Feldman (eds.), *The Dartmouth Bible* (2nd ed.; Boston: Houghton Mifflin Co., 1961), p. 146. See Numbers 1:50-54 for the functions of the Levites.

[27] George Sprau, *Literature in the Bible* (New York: Macmillan Co., 1932) p. 85.

[28] Nathaniel Micklem, Introduction to Leviticus, *The Interpreter's Bible*, II, 3.

[29] Chamberlin and Feldman, *op. cit.*, p. 118.

[30] John Marsh, Exegesis to Numbers, *The Interpreter's Bible*, II, 170.

[31] Charles Allen Dinsmore, *The English Bible as Literature* (Boston: Houghton Mifflin Co., 1931), p. 156.

[32] Divisions suggested by Ray Freeman Jenney, *Bible Primer* (New York: Harper & Brothers, 1955), pp. 35-36.

[33] Ernest S. Bates (ed.), *The Bible Designed to Be Read as Living Literature* (New York: Simon and Schuster, 1936), p. 120.

[34] Dinsmore, *op. cit.*, p. 157.

[35] Jenney, *op. cit.*, p. 39.

[36] Drawn chiefly from Chamberlin and Feldman, *op. cit.*, pp. 115, 118-119, and 150. See also *Webster's New International Dictionary*, 2nd ed., "Law," p. 1401.

[37] Jenney, *op. cit.*, p. 39.

[38] Sprau, *op. cit.*, p. 90.

[39] John Bright, Introduction to Joshua, *The Interpreter's Bible*, II, 548.

[40] Chase, *op. cit.*, pp. 100-101.

NOTES TO CHAPTER 4: RISE AND FALL OF THE MONARCHY

[1] See Jacob M. Myers, Introduction to the book of Judges, *The Interpreter's Bible* (Nashville, Tenn.: Abingdon Press, 1953), II, 677-682.

[2] See, for example, 2:11, 14 and 3:15.

[3] Mary Ellen Chase, *The Bible and the Common Reader* (rev. ed.; New York: Macmillan Co., 1952), pp. 103-105.

[4] Chase, *op. cit.*, 103-105.

[5] Jacob M. Myers, Exegesis to Judges, *The Interpreter's Bible*, II, 730.

[6] This element and the two following ones are all suggested by Wilbur Owen Sypherd, *The Literature of the English Bible* (New York: Oxford University Press, 1938), p. 61.

[7] S. R. Driver, *An Introduction to The Literature of the Old Testament*, (rev. ed.; New York: Charles Scribner's Sons, 1920), p. 168.

[8] Richard G. Moulton (ed.), *The Modern Reader's Bible* (New York: Macmillan Co., 1952), p. 1347.

[9] For a detailed discussion, see George B. Caird, Introduction and Exegesis to I and II Samuel, *The Interpreter's Bible*, II, 855-865. Most of the information in this Outline concerning the date and authorship of I and II Samuel is derived from Caird.

[10] Alice Parmelee, *A Guidebook to the Bible* (New York: Harper & Brothers, 1948), p. 26.

[11] For a list of the principal later additions, see Caird, Introduction, *The Interpreter's Bible*, II, 862-865.

[12] George Sprau, *Literature in the Bible* (New York: Macmillan Co., 1932), pp. 124-125.

[13] Title suggested by Ray Freeman Jenny, *Bible Primer* (New York: Harper and Brothers, 1955), p. 47.

[14] Title borrowed from Chase, *op. cit.*, p. 121.

[15] Chase, *op. cit.*, p. 122.

[16] See Caird, Introduction, *The Interpreter's Bible*, II, 863-864.

[17] Chase, *op. cit.*, pp. 133-134.

[18] See Caird, Exegesis, *The Interpreter's Bible*, II, 1059.

[19] Caird, Exegesis, *The Interpreter's Bible*, II, 1124-1125.

[20] There is some doubt whether there had ever been a promise. David seems to be confused and is convinced by Bathsheba and Nathan that he should favor Solomon's claims. See Norman H.

Snaith, Introduction and Exegesis to I and II Kings, *The Interpreter's Bible* (Nashville, Tenn.: Abingdon Press, 1954), III, 23-24.

[21] See Snaith, Exegesis, *The Interpreter's Bible*, III, 34.

[22] Most of the material for this section and that on the purpose and the method of the authors is based upon Snaith, Introduction, *The Interpreter's Bible*, III, 3-18.

[23] Sprau, *op. cit.*, p. 128.

[24] Snaith, Introduction, *The Interpreter's Bible*, III, 9-10. This procedure had to be abandoned, of course, after 722 B.C., when there were no longer any kings of Israel.

[25] Ernest Sutherland Bates (ed.), *The Bible Designed to Be Read as Living Literature* (New York: Simon and Schuster, 1936), p. 296.

[26] A contrary view of Solomon's wisdom is held by modern historians. Theodore H. Robinson says: "A wise man might have preserved and strengthened the new Israelite state, but Solomon was quite unfit for the task. Vain, ostentatious, shortsighted, selfish, and cowardly, he was unscrupulous in the attainment of his ends." ("The History of Israel," *The Interpreter's Bible* (Nashville, Tenn.: Abingdon Press, 1952), I, 282.

[27] The dates given in the parentheses refer to the years of the reign of each sovereign. These dates do not correspond exactly to those given by the Biblical historian but follow the chronology given by Harold H. Watts, in *The Modern Reader's Guide to the Bible* (rev. ed.; New York: Harper and Brothers, 1959), pp. 128-130. Robinson ("The History of Israel," *The Interpreter's Bible*, I, 282) gives the date of the death of Solomon and the accession of Rehoboam as 936 B.C.

[28] Frederick Carl Eiselen, Edwin Lewis, and David G. Downey (eds.), *The Abingdon Bible Commentary* (Nashville, Tenn.: Abingdon Press, 1929), p. 424.

[29] For a different conception of Jeroboam—as a good king who did what he thought was best for his people—see Eiselen, Lewis, and Downey, *op. cit.*, p. 424.

[30] The purpose in beautifying herself was probably to prepare her body for the next life. See Snaith, Exegesis, *The Interpreter's Bible*, III, 236.

[31] Snaith, Exegesis, *The Interpreter's Bible*, III, 194.

[32] Chase, *op. cit.*, p. 136.

[33] See *Ibid.*

[34] Chase, *op. cit.*, p. 139.

[35] Snaith, Exegesis, *The Interpreter's Bible*, III, 212.

[36] For a thorough discussion of the origin of Deuteronomic reform, see G. Ernest Wright, Introduction to Deuteronomy, *The Interpreter's Bible*, II, 323-326.

NOTES TO CHAPTER 5:
ESTABLISHMENT OF A CHURCH STATE AFTER THE EXILE

[1] Theodore H. Robinson, "The History of Israel," *The Interpreter's Bible* (Nashville, Tenn.: Abingdon Press, 1952), I, 287. The summary of the history of Palestine and the Hebrews included here is drawn chiefly from Robinson.

[2] George Sprau, *Literature in the Bible* (New York: Macmillan Co., 1932), pp. 124-125.

[3] For a detailed discussion of this vexing problem, see W. A. L. Elmslie, Introduction to I and II Chronicles, *The Interpreter's Bible* (Nashville, Tenn.: Abingdon Press, 1954), III, 345-347. Elmslie argues for an early date, *c.* 400-350. See also John Robinson Macarthur, *Biblical Literature and Its Backgrounds* (New York: Appleton-Century-Crofts, 1936), p. 175.

[4] It is believed that the Chronicler did not write these genealogies but began his narrative at 10:1. See Elmslie, Exegesis, The Interpreter's Bible, III, 349.

[5] Elmslie, Exegesis, *The Interpreter's Bible*, III, 349.

[6] For a full discussion of the sources, see Raymond A. Bowman, Introduction to Ezra and Nehemiah, *The Interpreter's Bible*, III, 554-560.

[7] Bowman, Introduction, *The Interpreter's Bible*, III, 555. Bowman places Neh. 7:1-73a in the Nehemiah narrative.

[8] For these and many more cogent arguments against the priority of Ezra, see Bowman, Introduction, *The Interpreter's Bible*, III, 562-563; and Roy B. Chamberlin and Herman Feldman (eds.), *The Dartmouth Bible* (rev. ed.; Boston: Houghton-Mifflin Co., 1961), p. 346. If Ezra preceded Nehemiah, then the order of the material, according to Professor Macarthur (*op. cit.*, pp. 185-186), should be as follows: Ezra 1:1-11; I Esdras 4:47b-56; I Esdras 4:62—5:6b; Ezra 2:1—8:36; Neh. 7:73b—8:18; Ezra 9:1—10:44; Neh. 9:1—10:39; Neh. 7:5—73a; Neh. 1:1—7:4; and Neh. 11:1—13:30.

[9] Approximately this arrangement is suggested by Bowman (Introduction, *The Interpreter's Bible*, III, 560).

[10] The Chronicler makes Sheshbazzar (Ezra 1:8) and Zerubbabel (Ezra 2:2) the same person. For a discussion of the matter, see Bowman, Exegesis, *The Interpreter's Bible*, III, 574-576.

[11] Chamberlin and Feldman, *op. cit.*, p. 837.

[12] *Ibid.*

NOTES TO CHAPTER 6: THE MACCABEAN REVOLT

[1] The facts in this table are drawn from Robert H. Pfeiffer, "The Literature and Religion of the Apocrypha," *The Interpreter's Bible*

(Nashville, Tenn.: Abingdon Press, 1952), I, 415-419. The dates given in Pfeiffer's article differ slightly from those given by Theodore H. Robinson, "The History of Israel," *The Interpreter's Bible*, I, 288-291.

2 Roy B. Chamberlin and Herman Feldman (eds.), *The Dartmouth Bible* (rev. ed.; Boston: Houghton Mifflin Co., 1961), p. 735.

3 *Ibid.*

4 Chamberlin and Feldman, *op. cit.*, p. 734.

5 Chamberlin and Feldman, *op. cit.*, pp. 765-766; and Harold H. Watts, *The Modern Reader's Guide to the Bible* (rev. ed.; New York: Harper and Brothers, 1959), p. 316.

6 See Chamberlin, and Feldman, *op. cit.*, pp. 734-735, 739, and 766; Wilbur Owen Sypherd, *The Literature of the English Bible* (New York: Oxford University Press, 1938), pp. 149-150; and Bruce M. Metzger, *An Introduction to the Apocrypha* (New York: Oxford University Press, 1957), p. 131.

7 Sypherd, *op. cit.*, p. 150; Chamberlin and Feldman, *op. cit.*, p. 739; and John Robertson Macarthur, *Biblical Literature and Its Backgrounds* (New York: Appleton-Century-Crofts, 1936), p. 358.

8 Chamberlin and Feldman, *op. cit.*, p. 739.

9 *Ibid.*

10 Chamberlin and Feldman, *op. cit.*, p. 767.

11 Macarthur (*op. cit.*, p. 359) suggests 125-75 B.C.; Sypherd (*op. cit.*, p. 150) places it "near the close of the first century B.C."; and Chamberlin and Feldman (*op. cit.*, p. 769) say that some authorities date the book *c.* 40 B.C.

12 John C. Thirlwall and Arthur Waldhorn (eds.), *A Bible for the Humanities* (New York: Harper and Brothers, 1954), p. 310.

Bibliography

REFERENCE WORKS

The Abingdon Bible Commentary. Nashville, Tenn.: Abingdon Press, 1929. Articles and commentaries on Biblical topics by a number of authorities.

Chamberlin, Roy B., and Herman Feldman, eds. *The Dartmouth Bible.* 2nd ed. Boston: Houghton Mifflin Co., 1961. An abridgment of the King James Version, with introductions, prefaces, notes, and annotated maps.

The Interpreter's Bible. 12 vols. Nashville, Tenn.: Abingdon Press, 1951-1957. The King James Version and the Revised Standard Version side by side, with an introduction, interpretation, and notes for each book of the Bible, general articles, and outline maps. 148 editors, consulting editors, and contributors, representing a cross section of Protestant scholarship.

The Interpreter's Dictionary of the Bible. Edited by George A. Buttrick. 4 vols. Nashville, Tenn.: Abingdon Press, 1962. Entries for Biblical persons, places, objects, terms, and doctrines. Maps and illustrations.

May, Herbert G., and Bruce M. Metzger, eds. *The Oxford Annotated Bible.* New York: Oxford University Press, 1962. The Revised Standard Version, with introductions, notes, general articles, and maps.

Miller, Madelaine S. and J. Lane. *Encylopedia of Bible Life.* Rev. ed. New York: Harper & Brothers, 1955.

———. *Harper's Bible Dictionary.* 6th ed. New York: Harper & Brothers, 1959.

New Analytical Indexed Bible. Chicago: John A. Dickson Co., 1931.

Westminister Dictionary of the Bible. Rev. ed. Philadelphia: Westminister Press, 1944.

THE BIBLE: GENERAL BOOKS

Bates, Ernest S., ed. *The Bible Designed To Be Read as Living Literature.* New York: Simon and Schuster, 1936.

Chase, Mary Ellen. *The Bible and the Common Reader*. Rev. ed. New York: Macmillan Co., 1952. Reprinted in paperback.

Dinsmore, Charles Allen. *The English Bible as Literature*. Boston: Houghton Mifflin Co., 1931.

Gardiner, J. H. *The Bible as English Literature*. New York: Charles Scribner's Sons, 1927.

Goodspeed, Edgar J. *How to Read the Bible*. Philadelphia: John C. Winston Co., 1946.

——, and J. M. Powis Smith, eds. *The Short Bible*. Chicago: University of Chicago Press, 1933. Reprinted by Modern Library (Random House).

Grant, Frederick C. *How To Read the Bible*. New York: Morehouse-Gorham Co., 1956.

Jenney, Ray Freeman. *Bible Primer*. New York: Harper & Brothers, 1955.

Keller, Werner. *The Bible as History*. Translated by William Neil. New York: William Morrow & Co., 1956.

Landis, Benson Y. *An Outline of the Bible, Book by Book*. New York: Barnes & Noble, Inc., 1963.

Macarthur, John R. *Biblical Literature and Its Backgrounds*. New York: Appleton-Century-Crofts, 1936.

Moulton, Richard G. *The Literary Study of the Bible*. Boston: D. C. Heath and Co., 1894.

Neil, William. *The Rediscovery of the Bible*. New York: Harper & Brothers, 1955.

Parmlee, Alice. *A Guidebook to the Bible*. New York: Harper & Brothers, 1948.

The Reader's Bible. New York: Oxford University Press, 1951.

Sprau, George. *Literature in the Bible*. New York: Macmillan Co., 1932.

Sypherd, Wilbur Owen. *The Literature of the English Bible*. New York: Oxford University Press, 1938.

Thirwall, John G., and Arthur Waldhorn, eds. *A Bible for the Humanities*. New York: Harper & Brothers, 1954.

Watts, Harold H. *The Modern Reader's Guide to the Bible*. Rev. ed. New York: Harper & Brothers, 1959.

Wild, Laura H. *A Literary Guide to the Bible*. New York: Harper & Brothers, 1922.

THE OLD TESTAMENT: GENERAL BOOKS

Bewer, Julius A. *The Literature of the Old Testament*. 3rd ed. rev. by Emil G. Kraeling. New York: Columbia University Press, 1962.

Chase, Mary Ellen. *Life and Language in the Old Testament*. New York: W. W. Norton & Co., 1955. Reprinted in paperback.

Driver, S. R. *An Introduction to the Literature of the Old Testament.* Rev. ed. New York: Charles Scribner's Sons, 1920. Reprinted in paperback by Meridian Books (World Publishing Co.).

Fowler, Henry T. *A History of the Literature of Ancient Israel.* New York: Macmillan Co., 1922.

Gaer, Joseph. *The Lore of the Old Testament.* Boston: Little, Brown and Co., 1952.

Heaton, E. W. *Everyday Life in Old Testament Times.* New York: Charles Scribner's Sons, 1956.

James, Fleming. *Personalities of the Old Testament.* New York: Charles Scribner's Sons, 1939.

Gottwald, Norman. *Light to the Nations: An Introduction to the Old Testament.* New York: Harper & Brothers, 1959.

Muilenburg, James. "The History of the Religion of Israel," *The Interpreter's Bible.* Nashville, Tenn.: Abingdon Press, 1952. I, 292-389.

Oesterley, W. O. E., and T. H. Robinson. *An Introduction to the Books of the Old Testament.* Greenwich, Conn.: Seabury Press, 1934.

Pfeiffer, Robert H. *Introduction to the Old Testament.* Rev. ed. New York: Harper & Brothers, 1948.

Robinson, Henry Wheeler. *Inspiration and Revelation in the Old Testament.* London: Oxford University Press, 1946. Reprinted in paperback.

Robinson, Theodore H. "The History of Israel," *The Interpreter's Bible.* Nashville, Tenn.: Abingdon Press, 1952. I, 272-291.

Rowley, H. H., ed. *The Old Testament and Modern Study: A Generation of Discovery and Research.* Oxford: Clarendon Press, 1951. Reprinted in paperback.

Schultz, Samuel J. *The Old Testament Speaks.* New York: Harper & Brothers, 1960.

CHAPTER 1: PALESTINE AND ITS PEOPLE

Albright, William F. "The Old Testament World," *The Interpreter's Bible.* Nashville, Tenn.: Abingdon Press, 1952. I, 233-271.

———. *From the Stone Age to Christianity.* Rev. ed. Baltimore, Md.: Johns Hopkins Press, 1957. Reprinted in paperback by Anchor Books (Doubleday).

Baly, Denis. *The Geography of the Bible.* New York: Harper & Brothers, 1957.

Browne, Lewis. *The Graphic Bible.* New York: Macmillan Co., 1928.

Burrows, Millar. *What Mean These Stones?* New Haven, Conn.: American Schools of Oriental Research, 1941. Reprinted in paperback by Meridian Books (World Publishing Co.).

De Vaux, Roland, *Ancient Israel: Its Life and Institutions*. Translated by John McHugh. New York: McGraw-Hill Book Co., 1961.

Finegan, Jack. *Light from the Ancient Past*. 2nd ed. Princeton, N. J.: Princeton University Press, 1959.

Finkelstein, Louis, ed. *The Jews: Their History, Culture, and Religion*. 2 vols. 3rd ed. New York: Harper & Brothers, 1949.

Gordon, Cyrus H. *World of the Old Testament*. Rev. ed. New York: Doubleday & Co., 1958.

Grant, Elihu. *The Orient in Bible Times*. Philadelphia: J. B. Lippincottt Co., 1920.

Grollenberg, L. B., ed. *Atlas of the Bible*. New York: Thomas Nelson and Sons, 1957.

Guignebert, Charles. *The Jewish World in the Time of Christ*. Translated by S. H. Hooke. New York: E. P. Dutton & Co., 1939.

Hurlbut, Jesse Lyman. *Bible Atlas*. Rev. ed. Chicago: Rand, McNally and Co., 1910.

Kenyon, Kathleen. *Archaeology in the Holy Land*. New York: Frederick A. Praeger, 1960. Reprinted in paperback.

———. *Digging up Jericho*. New York: Frederick A. Praeger, 1957.

May, Herbert, ed. *Oxford Bible Atlas*. New York: Oxford University Press, 1962.

Smith, George Adam. *The Historical Geography of the Holy Land*. 4th ed. New York: George H. Doran Co., 1896.

Wright, G. Ernest, and Floyd Vivian Filson, eds. *The Westminister Historical Atlas to the Bible*. Rev. ed. Philadelphia: Westminister Press, 1956.

———, and David Noel Freedman, eds. *The Bible Archaeologist Reader*. New York: Doubleday & Company, 1961. Paperback reprint of articles from *The Biblical Archaeologist*.

CHAPTER 2: THE NATURE, ORIGIN, AND CONTENTS OF THE BIBLE

Bruce, F. F. *The English Bible: A History of Translations from the Earliest English Versions to the New English Bible*. New York: Oxford University Press, 1961.

Bowie, Walter R. *The Story of the Bible*. Nashville, Tenn.: Abingdon Press, 1934.

Butterworth, Charles C. *The Literary Lineage of the King James Bible 1340-1611*. Philadelphia: University of Pennsylvania Press, 1941.

Colwell, Ernest C. *The Study of the Bible*. Chicago: University of Chicago Press, 1937.

Herklots, H. G. G. *How Our Bible Came to Us*. New York: Oxford University Press, 1954. Reprinted in paperback.

Jeffery, Arthur. "The Canon of the Old Testament," *The Interpreter's Bible*. Nashville, Tenn.: Abingdon Press, 1952. I, 32-45.

Kenyon, Frederic. *Our Bible and the Ancient Manuscripts*. Rev. ed. New York: Harper & Brothers, 1958.

Lewis, Frank Grant. *How the Bible Grew*. Chicago: University of Chicago Press, 1919.

MacGregor, Geddes. *The Bible in the Making*. Philadelphia: J. B. Lippincott Co., 1959.

Margolis, Max L. *The Hebrew Scriptures in the Making*. Philadelphia: Jewish Publication Society of America, 1922.

———. *The Story of Bible Translations*. Philadelphia: Jewish Publication Society of America, 1917.

O'Connell, John, ed. *The Holy Bible*. Chicago: The Catholic Press, 1950.

Price, Ira Maurice. *The Ancestry of Our English Bible*. 3rd ed. rev. by William A. Irwin and Allen P. Wikgren. New York: Harper & Brothers, 1956.

Pritchard, James Bennett, ed. *Ancient Near Eastern Texts Relating to the Old Testament*. Rev. ed. Princeton, N. J.: Princeton University Press, 1955.

Robinson, Henry W. *The Bible in Its Ancient and English Versions*. New York: Oxford University Press, 1954.

Rypins, Stanley. *The Book of Thirty Centuries*. New York: Macmillan Co., 1951.

Smyth, J. Paterson. *How We Got Our Bible*. Rev. ed. New York: Harper & Brothers, 1912.

Snaith, Norman H. "The Language of the Old Testament," *The Interpreter's Bible*. Nashville, Tenn.: Abingdon Press. I, 220-232.

Wikgren, Allen. "The English Bible," *The Interpreter's Bible*, I, 84-105.

CHAPTER 3: THE FOUNDING OF THE HEBREW NATION

Barrois, George A. "Chronology, Metrology, etc.," *The Interpreter's Bible*. Nashville, Tenn.: Abingdon Press, 1952. I, 142-164.

Bright, John. Introduction and Exegesis to Joshua, *The Interpreter's Bible*. Nashville, Tenn.: Abingdon Press, 1953. II, 541-550 and 553-573.

Buber, Martin. *Moses: The Revelation and the Covenant*. London: East & West Library, 1946. Reprinted in paperback by Torchbooks (Harper & Brothers).

Marsh, John. Exegesis to Numbers, *The Interpreter's Bible*. Nashville, Tenn.: Abingdon Pess, 1953. II, 142-308.

Meek, T. J. *Hebrew Origins*. Rev. ed. New York: Harper & Brothers, 1960. Reprinted in paperback.

Micklem, Nathaniel. Introduction to Leviticus, *The Interpreter's Bible*. Nashville, Tenn. Abingdon Press, 1953. II, 3-9.

Rowley, Harold H. *From Joseph to Joshua*. New York: Oxford University Press, 1950.

Rylaarsdam, J. Coert. Introduction and Exegesis to Exodus, *The Interpreter's Bible*. Nashville, Tenn.: Abingdon Press, 1952. I, 833-838 and 851-1099.

Simpson, Cuthbert A. Exegesis to Genesis, *The Interpreter's Bible*, I, 465-829.

———. "The Growth of the Hexateuch," The Interpreter's Bible, I, 185-200.

Wright, G. Ernest, Exegesis to Deuteronomy, *The Interpreter's Bible*, II, 331-537.

See also THE BIBLE: GENERAL BOOKS (p. 165) and THE OLD TESTAMENT: GENERAL BOOKS (p. 166).

CHAPTER 4: THE RISE AND FALL OF THE MONARCHY

Caird, George B. Introduction and Exegesis to I and II Samuel, *The Interpreter's Bible*. Nashville, Tenn.: Abingdon Press, 1953. II, 855-1176.

Muilenburg, James. "The History of the Religion of Israel," *The Interpreter's Bible*. Nashville, Tenn.: Abingdon Press, 1952. I, 305-335.

Myers, Jacob M. Introduction to Judges, *The Interpreter's Bible*, II, 677-687.

Robinson, Theodore. "The History of Israel," *The Interpreter's Bible*, I, 277-287.

Snaith, Norman H. Introduction and Exegesis to I and II Kings, *The Interpreter's Bible*. Nashville, Tenn.: Abingdon Pess, 1954. III, 3-338.

Szikszai, Stephen. *Story of Israel from Joshua to Alexander the Great*. Philadelphia: Westminister Press, 1960.

Welch, Adam C. *Kings and Prophets in Israel*. Nashville, Ill.: Alec R. Allenson, 1955.

See also THE BIBLE: GENERAL BOOKS (p. 165) and THE OLD TESTAMENT: GENERAL BOOKS (p. 166).

CHAPTER 5: ESTABLISHMENT OF A CHURCH STATE
AFTER THE EXILE

Bowman, Raymond A. Introduction and Exegesis to Ezra and Nehemiah, *The Interpreter's Bible*. Nashville, Tenn.: Abingdon Press, 1954. III, 551-819.

Elmslie, W. A. L. Introduction and Exegesis to I and II Chronicles, *The Interpreter's Bible*, III, 341-548.

Goodspeed, E. J. *The Story of the Apocrypha*. Chicago: University of Chicago Press, 1939.

Metzger, Bruce M. *An Introduction to the Apocrypha*. New York: Oxford University Press, 1957.

Muilenburg, James. "The History of the Religion of Israel," *The Interpreter's Bible*. Nashville, Tenn.: Abingdon Press, 1952. I, 335-340.

Pfeiffer, Robert H. "The Literature and Religion of the Apocrypha," *The Interpreter's Bible*, I, 391-419.

Robinson, Theodore. "The History of Israel," *The Interpreter's Bible*, I, 287-288.

See also THE BIBLE: GENERAL BOOKS (p. 165) and THE OLD TESTAMENT: GENERAL BOOKS (p. 166).

CHAPTER 6: THE MACCABEAN REVOLT

Charles, R. H. *Religious Development between the Old and the New Testaments*. New York: Oxford University Press, 1914.

Farmer, W. R. *Maccabees, Zealots, and Josephus: An Inquiry into Jewish Nationalism*. New York: Columbia University Press, 1956.

Goodspeed, Edgar J. *The Story of the Apocrypha*. Chicago: University of Chicago Press, 1939.

Metzger, Bruce M. *An Introduction to the Apocrypha*. New York: Oxford University Press, 1957.

Pfeiffer, Robert H. *History of New Testament Times: With an Introduction to the Apocrypha*. New York: Harper & Brothers, 1949.

Robinson, Theodore H. "The History of Israel," *The Interpreter's Bible*. Nashville, Tenn.: Abingdon Press, 1952. I, 288-291.

See also THE BIBLE: GENERAL BOOKS (p. 165).

Index

173

Maccabeans, Maccabees, 10, 146, 147, 149. *See also* Judas Maccabeus

Maccabees (I and II, books), 17, 18, 24, 25, 42, 67, 148-156

Macduff, 97

Macedonia, rule over Palestine, 9-10, 145

Machir (tribe), 83

Magnificat, 92

Major Prophets, 17

Malachi, 122

Malachi (book), 17, 28, 29, 122

Mamre, 51

Manasseh (king), 71, 113, 129, 130

Manasseh (son of Joseph), 55, 58

Manasseh (tribe), 7, 75, 83, 135

Manna, 62

Manoah, 87

Marah, 62

Mark (Gospel), 18, 55, 122

Martin, Gregory, 31

Mary (Mother of Jesus), 92

Mary I (Tudor), 29, 31

Masoretes, 20, 21

Masoretic text, 20, 35, 38

Mattaniah, 113, 130

Mattathias (father of Judas Maccabeus), 10, 146, 149-150, 151

Mattathias (son of Simon), 152

Matthew, 15

Matthew (Gospel), 15, 17, 18, 65, 122

Matthew, Thomas, 28

Matthew Bible, 28, 29

Meek, T. J., 39

Megiddo, 84

Megilloth, 17

Melchishua, 97

Melkart, 117

Menahem, 115

Menelaus (priest), 154

Mephibosheth, 100, 104

Merab, 99

Merneptah, 6

Merom, 79

Messiah, 14, 22, 98, 122

Methuselah, 48-49

Micaiah, 119, 120

Michal, 96, 97, **101-102**

Michelangelo, 65

Midianites, defeat by Gideon, 84-85

Milcom, 110

Milton, John, 87

Minor Prophets, 17, 20

Miriam, 58, 59, 69

Mizpah, 95

Moabites, origin of, 52

Modern Douay Bible, 34, **36-37**

Modern Hebrew Bible, 35

Moffatt, James, 38

Moffatt Bible, 35, **38**, 39

Molech, 110

Moses, 6, 12, 44, 45, **58-75**, 76, 79, 122, 125, 128, 130, 141, 142, 147; birth of, 58-59; Blessing of, 75; call of, 59-60; death of, 75; exile of, 59; Last Song of, 74; as leader of Hebrew Exodus, 61-75; plagues on Egypt brought by, 60-61; Ten Commandments and other laws received by, 62-63

Mount. *See* name of mountain, such as Carmel, Sinai, etc.

Naaman, 126, 127

Naboth, 114, 120, 121, **124**

Nabunaid, 132

Nadab, 114

Naphtali, 55

Naphtali (tribe), 75, 183

Nathan, 101, 102, 103, 105

Nazarite (Nazirite), 67

Nebo, Mount, 75

Nebuchadrezzar, 2, 20, 111, 113, **130-131**, 132, 138, 144

Nehemiah, 9, 43, 133, **139-141**, 142, 143

Nehemiah (book), 16, 25, 132, 133, **136-142**

New English Bible, 40-41

Nicanor, 146, 151, 155, 156

Nicanor's Day, 146, 151, 153, 156

Nicholas of Hereford, 27

Nineveh, 9

Noah, 14, **48-50**